Overcoming Memory Problems

About the authors

Robert Erdmann, Ph.D., an American psychologist and nutrition expert who moved to the UK in 1986, runs a clinic in Tunbridge Wells specializing in biochemical testing and counselling. He was for nine years in Research and Development for the USAF in human capabilities and functioning, and for 20 years with IBM as Staff and Research Psychologist. He is the author of a number of books.

Meirion Jones is a freelance journalist with special interest in health issues, and has worked with Robert Erdmann on most of his books.

Overcoming Memory Problems

What to do to combat forgetfulness and memory loss

Robert Erdmann Ph.D. and Meirion Jones

THORSONS PUBLISHING GROUP

First published in 1990

Copyright © Robert Erdmann and Meirion Jones 1990

British Library Cataloguing in Publication Data
Erdmann, Robert
Overcoming Memory Problems: what to do to combat
forgetfulness and memory loss.
1. Man. Memory. Neuropsychological aspects
I. Title   II. Jones, Meirion
153.1

ISBN 0 7225 1961 3

Published by Thorsons Publishers Limited, Wellingborough,
Northamptonshire NN8 2RQ, England

Typeset by Trintype, Wellingborough
Printed in Great Britain by Mackays, Chatham, Kent

1 3 5 7 9 10 8 6 4 2

Contents

1

Echoes of the Mind

Oliver, a salesman in his mid-thirties, is driving through Dorset, in the south of England. He works for a company which develops specialist software for the business community and has just clinched a deal with a large firm of lawyers in Exeter. With a few hours to kill, and feeling extremely pleased with himself, he has chosen a detour through the downs of Thomas Hardy country instead of returning straight up the motorway to his company's offices in Swindon.

It is a glorious day. He winds back the sunroof of his car and feels the warm wind ruffle his hair. As the tranquil hedgerows and pastures roll by, he thinks about the forthcoming holiday in the Seychelles with his wife. He has exceeded his sale targets by miles and the commission on the Exeter deal alone will pay for the loft conversion. Andy and Sue are coming for dinner this evening, he remembers. They must fix up a game of squash. Life is pretty good right now.

Suddenly, his mood changes. His throat tightens and a small moan involuntarily escapes his lips. Tears form in his eyes, blurring the road ahead and he is forced to pull over onto the verge. As he switches off the engine, a wave of sadness swells over him. His morning's achievements, the prospective holiday, the loft conversion, all seem meaningless, their ability to thrill him suddenly drained. He feels an overwhelming sense of loss, as if something irreplaceable has been snatched away – as if he has been bereaved. What has triggered this dramatic change of mood? His bewilderment at its apparent lack of cause only heightens his misery.

We'll leave Oliver for the moment, with the promise of solving this little emotional mystery in due course.

In the meantime, let's turn our attention elsewhere, and watch a woman as she walks along a hospital corridor to the door of a private room. Inside, her husband sits by his bed, his concentration wholly absorbed by a game of patience. As the woman enters, his face lights up, in an expression of joy and surprise. He jumps to his feet and embraces her passionately. 'Darling,' he cries, 'it's so good to see you.'

'Do you love me?' she asks.

'Of course I do. You know I do,' he answers assuredly. He holds her hands to his lips and kisses them very hard.

They sit down together on the bed. She pauses, then asks: 'Have you ever seen me before?'

'No,' he replies with the same firmness. 'You're the first person I've ever seen in my life. Why haven't I seen you before?' He takes a drink from a cup on his bedside table. 'This is the first cup of coffee I have ever tasted. I am conscious for the first time.' Lying on the bed next to his playing cards is the man's diary – a lined exercise book. The wife picks it up and turns the pages. The most recent entry echoes what he has just said: 'I am truly alive for the first time.' However, each preceding line carries an almost identical sentence – with the exception that the word 'truly' has been scribbled out with every succeeding entry.

This extraordinary scene sounds like a surreal nightmare, with its commonplace language rendered incomprehensible by the disturbing contradictions. Yet the circumstances are only too real. Three years ago, this man fell victim to herpes simplex encephalitis – a virus similar to the one which causes the common cold sore, except that in this case it attacks the brain rather than the lips. The virus destroyed crucial brain structures called the hippocampus and temporal lobes. It is these mechanisms within the brain which store our conscious memories – providing us with the ability to recall past events and experiences and relate them to our present. Without these memory components, life for this man has become a single moment of awareness frozen into infinity. He might see or hear something, read a book, taste a cup of coffee, smell a scent, but, having no means of storing, and subsequently remembering, these events, they will instantly fade from his consciousness. Consequently, he is damned to live his life as if he were perpetually awakened newly born.

And yet despite the complete absence of conscious memory, he is still able to speak, to write, to play patience, to recognize his wife and feel profound love for her, even though he cannot remember her name, even though each time he sees her it is the first time he has ever seen her. This raises fascinating questions about the nature of memory, the way it stores impressions and the way it recalls them. It also underlines in the cruellest way possible how important memory is. More than sight or hearing, or the use of our limbs, memory is what links us to the world. Lose your memory and you have lost the world.

The future shaper

The brain is a magpie's nest and the memory is the treasure trove contained within it. Every waking second of the day a hoard of new booty – scavenged from the kaleidoscope of faces, words, noises, music fragments, names, buildings, timetables, emotions, sound bites, soap operas, perfumes, colours and cravings that swirl around us – is crammed into the nest and tucked away in its recesses for future use. It is the ability first to store, and then to recreate, these events in our minds that allows us to adapt and learn from changing environments.

Paradoxically, therefore, by giving us access to our past, it is our memories that forge our future. Look again at the man in the hospital room. Robbed of his memories, and of his abilities to learn from his experiences, he is like a walker lost in a landscape devoid of any recognizable features. For without memories – the recognizable landmarks of the mind – we are incapable of taking our bearings, of calculating where we stand in the world. The only way we can react to, and understand, each new experience is by comparing it to ones we have already had and with which we are familiar – just as the walker compares landmarks with those on his map. Without the benefit of previous experiences, therefore, new ones are meaningless.

A walk into memory

So how should memories work for us? How does this 'mind gap' operate? Let's find out by watching our friend Oliver, this time as a youth of nineteen. He is on holiday, his first without his parents, in a popular seaside resort. As we zoom in, he is walking along the Georgian esplanade, wearing his 1973-style Bermuda shorts. Even for walking, this simplest of actions, his memory operates on many levels. At the deepest, most instinctive level, far out of reach of conscious control, the brain is sending messages to the heart telling it to beat faster so that a more rapid blood flow will provide extra oxygen for the muscles. It also orders the diaphragm to rise and fall more frequently so that his breathing is quicker and more oxygen is made available for the stronger circulation. Blood vessels in the leg muscles are dilated so that more oxygen reaches muscle cells, while for non-essential organs, such as the stomach, blood is diverted causing his digestion rate to slow down.

Higher up, on an unconscious level, where remembered actions have become acquired reflexes through many years of repetition, the brain provides the muscles with instructions on how to walk briskly and upright. Muscles are constantly flexed and relaxed. Just the right pressure is applied through the toes to keep balance, with minor adjustments being made to the amount of pressure on the levers of the bones and muscles. The brain also fixes the eyes on a landmark, rolling them in their sockets against the movement of the body so that, to Oliver, his surroundings don't appear to rise and fall disconcertingly.

And now we turn to the high, conscious, level of memory. As he walks down the street, Oliver sees a figure walking towards him. Immediately, his brain starts decoding impressions of the approaching figure by referring them to previously acquired stores of memory. The figure's shape – hips, breasts, hair – confirm that it is female. Closer, and the more specific identification of facial features – bone structure, lips, eyes, forehead – passes to the brain where they are cross-referenced against stored memories. The face is recognized, in turn providing a series of other memories – her name, her age, occupation and relationship to the man. Perhaps fragments of past conversations and shared experiences are turned up.

Nearer still and Oliver experiences a sense of alarm – which a split second later he realizes is caused by an absence of make-up on her face. Again this impression results from the brain cross-referencing incoming stimuli against remembered information. A conversation is recalled: 'You'll know when I'm really angry 'cos I won't feel like wearing make-up.' The girl's lips are pursed grimly, her eyelids narrowed, a frown knits her brows. Instantly, Oliver's brain – searching through its recall of similar experiences – unravels the cause of the anger and aggression by triggering recent memories of love entreaties to this girl, of earnest discussion of marriage, and of subsequent betrayal, of falling instead for the girl's best friend.

Now the two are only feet apart, her pace quickens and she lunges at him, lifting her hand to slap his face. Instinctively he flinches, bringing up his hand to protect himself.

Even in this simplest of examples, therefore, memory is working non-stop: receiving fresh stimuli – the sight of the girl, the signs of her anger, and so on – and interpreting their meaning by referring them to memories of previous related events. At the same time, the body is guided by other brain responses: the instinctive ducking away from her blow; the near-instinctive interpretation of the anger on her face; the conscious, long-term memory of her face and personality; and the newer memories of the guilty two-timing. So, even though this particular situation is probably unique – nothing exactly like it having occurred before – it is made from a jigsaw puzzle, whose separate parts correspond to experiences similar to those which have occurred in the past. By revisiting the past through his memory, therefore, Oliver's present is explained to him.

Memory works like this in everything we do. Using our senses – sight, hearing, smell, touch and taste – to hoard the hundreds of instantly occurring experiences, it makes sense of them by referring them to past experiences. Driving a car, writing, speaking, loving, all require this complex, instantaneous referral to millions of past experiences to enable us to perform them.

Which brings us back to the amnesiac in the hospital room. Cast adrift in a world where with each second he experiences the world afresh; yet, having no means of storing the experience, he has to repeat it forever. Of course, this is the most extreme case possible, and few people are unlucky enough to be so severely affected. But memory loss has many different causes and degrees of severity. Certain levels of memory can be damaged while others remain untouched. So, while this man –

as crippled by his inability to store memories as he is – retains his intelligence, other victims of memory loss can degenerate to a state where they lose control even of those actions most of us use purely instinctively. The senile dementia which is symptomatic of Alzheimer's disease, for example, causes incontinence, an inability to eat, an almost complete loss of awareness. And between these extremes of amnesia and senility lie varying disturbing degress of memory loss and forgetfulness.

Memories in the future

In future chapters, we'll be looking at each cause of memory loss. We'll examine the controversy surrounding the presence of aluminium in the environment and the way it is thought to exacerbate Alzheimer's disease; we'll also look at the nutritional causes of memory loss.

We also examine ways and means of combating loss of memory using a well-stocked armoury of preventive measures, depending on the source of the problem. These range from mnemonics and other techniques for making the most of your memory, to specifically constructed diets and means of avoiding many of the factors that contribute to a decline in retentive ability. Finally, the last chapter contains information on how to cope should a loved one fall victim to Alzheimer's disease.

Before all this, though, let's start by seeing how the whole thing works.

The memory mechanism – part one

The average brain weighs about 3 pounds (1.5 kg). However, this tiny amount – approximately 2 per cent of overall body weight – is the centre of 25 per cent of all metabolic activity, consuming a quarter of the oxygen and food carried around the body in the bloodstream. Such a seemingly enormous imbalance between size and energy consumption is a clue to just how powerful the memory is. Chemical activity in the body – such as the creation of enzymes and hormones, cell growth and the constriction of muscles – requires energy to power it. The greater the chemical reaction, the more energy is consumed to drive it. Since more energy is spent powering the brain than the heavy, physically active muscles of our limbs, then the brain must be the centre of quite phenomenal biochemical activity. This activity essentially concerns the relay of messages around the body. In order to understand the workings of the memory – and how things can go wrong with it – it's important to see how this relay system operates. First of all, read the following heading very carefully before submitting it to your memory.

Compact discs and alchemy

The brain, the spinal cord and its nerve fibres which endlessly subdivide off from its trunk into a network that suffuses to the farthest tips of the body, are made up of specially adapted cells called neurons. It is the neurons which carry messages from our sense organs to the brain, constantly appraising it of what is happening around the body. The same neurons then relay the brain's response to these messages (such as recognizing the girlfriend and ducking her blow).

How are these messages conveyed? After all, when we respond to a stimulus – such as the sight of the girlfriend's face – it isn't as if that face were passing through the eye to be projected onto a screen at the back of the skull. Instead, every external stimulus, sight, hearing, taste, touch and smell, has to be translated into a special code suitable for travel along the neurons.

This translation from external stimulus to coded nerve impulse is a remarkable process. In the Dark Ages, alchemists dreamed of discovering a substance that would miraculously transform base metal into gold. This transforming element – the philosopher's stone – was greatly revered and looked upon as a source of fantastic power. Unwittingly, the alchemists could have invented a metaphor for one of the most important functions in the body.

The truth is, we each possess the philosopher's stone. It is carried around by our bodies in the form of highly sensitive nerve cells which line the retina, inner ear, nasal passages, skin and every area of the body, acting as an 'interface' between the world without and within. The 'alchemical' nature of these cells is provided by substances formed from polyunsaturated fatty acids. Most people will only have heard of this term by reading the ingredients list on lids of margarine tubs. Unlike the contents of margarine, whose goodness is largely destroyed by industrial food processing, in our bodies essential polyunsaturates are chemicals of fantastic importance. They attract oxygen very readily, causing a variety of reactions from determining the health of cell membranes and regulating blood cholesterol levels to fighting cancer.

Polyunsaturated fatty acids are also finely-honed biochemical tuning forks. When struck, an ordinary tuning fork emits a clear tone, having converted one form of energy, kinetic, to another, sound. This conversion process is called transduction. Similarly, when the polyunsaturate-rich neurons come into contact with external stimuli such as sights and sounds, these stimuli are themselves transduced, converted from light or sound waves into electrical impulses. It is these impulses which then pass up the neurons to the brain in a wave of polarized ions.

Perhaps the closest comparison between this and the everyday world is to look at the way in which a piece of music is put onto compact disc. To do this, live music is fed into a digital encoder and transformed into a series of numbers. This is a digital code unique to that sound. It will later be read by a laser beam in the compact disc player and the music reconstructed so precisely that it sounds clearer. As with the CD, so with the nerves. Once the polyunsaturate-enriched cells – the body's very own digital encoders – have transduced the stimulus, it then passes to the brain, where the impulses will be read and a copy of the stimulus reconstructed.

Junctions and gulfs

Unfortunately, while the encoding of the message is similar to the making of a CD, the way it is relayed to the brain cannot be compared to the transmission of music from amplifier to speakers. The relay of the nerve impulse is not a steady, uninterrupted flow. Rather, the impulse must pass along a line of thousands of separate cells that pave its route to the brain, each of which is separated by a gap called a synapse which the impulse must somehow cross. Rather than making up a continuous line, the nerve fibres are divided into these separate cells for a very good reason. For rather than constituting simple, undeviating pathways, each nerve fibre is part of a massive, meshed network of interconnections. Nerves carrying messages from outlying parts of the body meet up with others, merging into larger and larger fibres until finally meeting the spinal cord. Each cell, therefore, acts not only as a relay for its own messages but as a junction for others arriving from separate routes – in much the same way that a country's road network is made of lots of small roads which meet at crossroads, T-junctions and roundabouts. The synapse, therefore, acts as a biochemical 'give way' sign.

So how does the message cross this synapse? In the past, the transmission of impulse across the synaptic gulf has been likened to a spark erupting from a plug in the ignition of a car engine. In fact, for a very good reason, this is far from the truth. Remember, the routes along these nerve branches might be carrying many messages at once. If the only medium required to pass the messages from one cell to the next was an indiscriminate spark, the receiving cell would be unable to distinguish between one message and another. All it would pick up would be scrambled biochemical static.

What happens instead is much more subtle. Let's watch a single message passing through a neuron. We see it approaching the neuron's farthermost tip – a structure called an axon which protudes from the body of the cell like a snail's horn into the empty gulf of the synapse. As the message touches it, the axon secretes a special chemical into the synapse. This bridges the gulf and creates a chemical reaction in the dendrite – or receiving structure – on the next cell. The reaction then stimulates an identical message to pass through to this second cell's axon, and so on up to the brain.

The bridging substance secreted by the axon is called a neurotransmitter. Forty of these neurotransmitters have so far been identified and their chemical structures vary depending on the message being conveyed. They can be made of a variety of amino acids (the building blocks of protein), amines (chemical compounds made from amino acids), polyunsaturated fatty acids, hormones and enzymes. Some are widely known such as the excitory neurotransmitter, adrenalin, and L-dopa, a substance used widely to treat victims of Parkinson's disease.

Others such as serotonin and acetylcholine are rarely mentioned outside the laboratory. But each and every neurotransmitter is crucial to our story – to the ways in which memory can be prolonged, protected and improved, as well as the ways in which it can become vulnerable to damage, disease and amnesia. They play major roles in the biochemical processes of memory and learning and we'll return to look at them many times throughout the book.

How the brain solves its traffic problem

We've just looked at the passage of one nerve message across two neurons from one axon to the next dendrite. In reality, these cells receive as many as ten thousand different messages at a time and convey them across separate synaptic connections to adjacent cells. Think of the interconnecting neurons as the motorways of a vast and populous country, the messages as the traffic that plies them, and the brain as a vast conurbation at the hub of this activity. It paints a picture of such congestion that London on railstrike day must seem like a deserted moor. With so much information being passed to the brain to be processed and orders being sent out in response, how can the brain possibly cope? Why does it not just snarl up?

With upwards of three million vehicles on London's roads, it stands to reason that it would only take three million separate routes into the city, giving each car a route to itself, to clear the congestion completely. The secret to avoiding brain congestion, then, must be to have as many routes around the brain as there are nerve messages. So how many does the brain have? To start with, the brain contains at least 15 billion neurons. Each of these has the capacity to link up with not one or two neighbours but 10,000. This means that there are potentially 150,000,000,000,000 (150 trillion) separate routes for the messages to take! In terms of information, this is roughly equivalent to 750 million books the length of this one. Little wonder that scientists claim that a great proportion of our brain capacity remains unused.

The memory mechanism – part two

So far we've seen how the stimuli that cram our waking lives to bursting point are converted into nerve messages, then transmitted to the brain. That's the easy part. What we must do now is see how these messages are stored in the brain as memories. After all, if the only thing these messages did once they reached the brain was pass ineffectively from one cell to the next, eventually fading like an echo in a cavern, they would have little use. The fact that these messages are stored suggests that a mechanism exists for imprinting them on the brain, that when an impulse reaches it, a physical change occurs in the brain which stores them – a change, moreover, which it might be possible to measure.

The question of just what this mechanism is, and what sort of change occurs, has fascinated and inspired philosophers for thousands of years. Early theories – lacking the basis of advanced surgical and psychological expertise – tried to define the factors which trigger memory rather than what memory itself is. Nevertheless, these theories are very useful for helping us to understand how memory affects our behaviour. Aristotle, for example, divided memory into two categories. There was, he said, the memory common to all animals which gave them the instincts necessary for hunting for food and rearing young. Then there was the memory peculiar to humans which enables us to sense the passing of time, and to draw conclusions by linking past experiences and relating them to current conditions. Modern psychologists now see the differentiation between humans and animals as a matter of degree rather than absolute since tests show that animals are also capable of linking previous experiences to current situations. (Many of these tests are tremendously important to our understanding of memory and we'll be referring to them shortly.)

Aristotle also defined ways in which memory was triggered through four associations. These were caused by linking:

1 events or objects that were related geographically – the sea andits shoreline, for example
2 events that occurred more or less simultaneously, such as a breaking wave and the sound it makes as it crashes
3 events or objects that are similar in some feature, such as the sea and a lake
4 events or objects that trigger the memory because they

contrast with each other, such as the sea and the desert.

In the late nineteenth century, American psychologist James D. Weinland added a further four associations to Aristotle's original quartet. These were:

5 cause and effect. Swimming in the sea, for example, will make you wet
6 part and whole, such as wave and ocean
7 particular and general, such as Brighton beach and the Atlantic ocean
8 numerical contiguity – such as the seven seas.

Looking at memories in terms of these multiple associations, they can be seen as entries in a gigantic reference library – one, don't forget, that holds 750 million books (pity the poor librarian). Each subject, like our example of the sea, has numerous cross-linkages thanks to the different means of triggered associations.

Which brings us quite neatly back to Oliver. You may remember, we left him sitting forlornly at the wheel of his car, feeling pretty sorry for himself. For a full five minutes he sits there, then, decisively, he climbs out into the sunlight and, walking along the shimmering tarmac, retraces his route to the point in the road where his mood inexplicably changed. At that point he notices a gap in the tall hedgerow. This gives an uninterrupted view of the lowest point where two hills meet, beyond which, sparkling in the sun, lies the sea. The flat, pebbly swath of Chesil beach arcs round to meet Portland, a blurred, blue wedge on the horizon. Suddenly the memories of his holiday flood back. The view, he realizes, is almost identical to the one from the esplanade of the town where he stayed. Even though he hadn't consciously noticed it as he drove past, it registered on a subliminal level, triggering the bittersweet emotions of lost love and guilty betrayal.

All is revealed. He laughs, trots back to his car and drives off into a commission-packed future.

As for us, we've seen only the tip of the memory iceberg. Having discovered the way in which recollections can be triggered – and still remembering that sub-heading from page 13 – let's turn our attention to the way in which they are stored.

2

Etching the Echo

In Chapter 1 we saw how external stimuli such as the innumerable sights, sounds and smells that constantly envelop our lives are transformed by the polyunsaturate-enriched nerve cells into electrical impulses. We then watched as these were transmitted to the brain – with the help of specially adapted chemicals called neurotransmitters to help bridge the synapses. Once in the brain, the impulses were filed away as memories in a gargantuan reference library where they would wait until called upon to supply the body with guidance on how to react in given situations.

However, while we've seen how messages are passed to the brain, and the psychological triggers which are used to recall them from the 'files', what we have yet to do is explain the actual process itself. In order for a memory to be stored, it is generally agreed that a physical change has to occur in the brain. Whatever the process is which imprints that memory, the end result must be every bit as tangible as an etching on a copper plate or a painting on a canvas. Somehow, or other, the structure of the brain itself has to change to accommodate new memories and thus prevent such memories from fading into nothing. So what can this physical change be? This is what we'll attempt to find out.

The source of memory

It was while operating on the temporal lobes of epilepsy victims that the American neurosurgeon and psychologist, Wilder Penfield, made a remarkable discovery. Performing brain surgery on one such patient who was at the time conscious but under local anaesthetic, he prodded a section of her brain with a probe.

Simultaneously, the patient claimed she heard music – clearly, distinctly, as if it were in the room. After a few seconds, she said the sound faded. Then Penfield repeated the prodding and the woman again heard the piece of music, indeed, the same passage. After the operation, the woman realized the music was a piece she had been very fond of in her youth. Yet she hadn't even given it a thought for years.

Excited by the implications of this discovery, Penfield extended his research. By stimulating different areas of his patients' brains with small electrical currents, he was able to cause vivid recollections of forgotten experiences to surface in their consciousnesses with extraordinary clarity. These findings seemed to suggest, remarkably, that individual memories were stored in highly specific, compact portions of the brain. The woman's memory of the music, for example, would seem to have been stored in only a few cells of the entire brain.

A quick circuit of the brain

From Penfield's findings, the argument for memories occupying small, localized compartments seemed conclusive. Then another leading American psychologist, Karl Lashley, unexpectedly developed a quite different theory. Using a group of laboratory mice, Lashley taught them to find food hidden in the heart of a complex maze. At first, the mice had great difficulty finding their way around and became easily confused and disorientated. Gradually, though, by acclimatizing themselves to their environment – working out the spatial relationship between one passageway and another, whether a right turning would then lead to a left – the mice learnt to find their way around the maze to reach the food at its centre.

Lashley then began to remove portions of their temporal lobes. These were the areas responsible for storing their memories of the maze and the portions which Penfield had correspondingly operated on in his human patients. Remarkably, removing up to a fifth of the overall brain tissue didn't seem to affect the mice's memories in the least. They found their way to the food as effortlessly as before. It was only as he removed more of their brain tissue that their memories started to decline. Even then the loss of memory was only progressive rather than sudden

– with the mice taking longer to find their way about or becoming confused at certain corners. Yet, according to Penfield's work, since memory was stored in small, highly localized areas, removal of such an area would either have no effect or cause a total loss of memory. But here were the mice demonstrating only partial memory loss.

Lashley's conclusions dramatically contradicted Penfield's. The experiment with the mice suggested that every memory is spread out through the entire brain in a complicated pattern, or that the same memory is mirrored time and again throughout the brain. Of these two ideas, Lashley plumped for the first. He conceived of a process whereby the storage of impressions in the brain occurred by linking many neurons together in a sort of circuit. Therefore, even if some neurons were removed, as with his mice experiment, the circuit would remain partially intact, leaving memory only partially impeded.

The idea of a memory as a brain circuit – or 'engram' as Lashley called it – is the most commonly held theory today. Each stimulus, as it is received by the brain, is said to create an engram which may extend like a meandering stream from one end of the temporal lobe to the other.

Reverberations and microchips

Among the most prominent psychologists to share Lashley's theory is the Canadian, Donald Hebb. He believes that external stimuli create 'reverberations' within the brain which outlast the stimuli and that it is these reverberations which create the circuits. The idea of a reverberation echoing around the brain is itself only a metaphor to explain a process which is, as yet, inexplicable (similar to the mediaeval alchemists' descriptions of the philosopher's stone, perhaps?). No one really knows yet why a circuit will form in the way it does. And there is always the possibility that the particular shape of a circuit is quite arbitrary.

However, while the question of how such a circuit comes about remains clouded in mystery, there is little doubt today that this is the way memory is stored. Computers, radios, televisions and most other modern electrical appliances store much of their information in a similar way. The ubiquitous silicon chip, for example, is a circuit board onto which are printed minute fragments of separate information. These fragments are individually meaningless. However, when connected by an electrical current to each other via the circuitry, they produce quite complex commands. In the same way, individual neurons connect together to form a memory.

Strengthening the circuit

Of course, the brain circuits, engrams, are almost infinitely more complex than the microchip. The engram also differs from the microchip in that when it is first formed, it is remarkably fragile and unstable. If not reinforced, then the engram may simply break up again into its separate neuron components. This is because, when the engram is first formed to record an impression it is as part of what is called the short term, or labile, memory. The short term has a life of only a few seconds and scientists think that when an impression is first stored as a memory, the physical links between each neuron in the engram are weak and unformed. It is only through repeated exposure to that impression that the links grow stronger – transferring the engram from a short term memory to a long term memory.

You can see a classic illustration of the fragility of the engram links of short term memory when you phone directory enquiries for a phone number. Let us assume there is no pen handy so that you have to remember the number when it is given to you rather than being able to write it down. The operator gives you the number you want and rings off. Unless you recite the number to yourself time and time again, it is more likely that your memory of the number will disappear within a few seconds or, at best, that you only remember some numbers from the sequence.

However, after repeating the number to yourself for a minute or two, the likelihood will be much greater of your subsequently being able to remember that number. This is because repeating the number time and time again has strengthened the physical links between the cells of that particular engram. A useful comparison is to imagine drawing a very faint line with a soft pencil. This near-invisible line is the short term memory of your phone number. Every time you retrace your pencil over that line, though, no matter how softly you press, the line becomes thicker, darker and more permanent. In the same way, each time you repeat that phone number – by reciting it or redialling it – the stimuli reactivates the same circuit of cells in the brain. This in turn reinforces the links between the individual cells in the circuit.

This reinforcing process is known as consolidation. It is a gradual structural change which, in terms of our memorized telephone numbers, shifts it from the ephemerality of short term memory to the concrete permanency of long term memory. Just how ephemeral the short term memory is has been demonstrated by experiments designed to interfere with the initial storage. When volunteers are given a phone number to remember, they are interrupted by being made to recite other, meaningless numbers at short intervals. In this way, the memory of the phone number disappears almost immediately, as if the engram were being broken up by the invading impressions of these other numbers.

The short term memory's fragility is further emphasized by examining the cases of victims of head injuries. Very often these victims are unable to remember the events that occurred to them in the hours or days before the injury, while having perfect recall of events that happened further back. This suggests a time element involved in the transition of memory from short to long term, and that if the engram were interrupted before proper consolidation takes place, then the memory disappears.

The memory resistance

What exactly is the mechanism that enables separate neurons to form an engram, this strange 'reverberating' brain circuit? As you may remember from Chapter 1, each neuron is separated from contact with its 10,000 or so potential neighbours by synapses. Messages are conveyed from one cell to the next across the synapse by neurotransmitters. Synapses play a vital role in channelling the millions of nerve impulses towards the brain. However, because of their very nature – they are, after all, a physical gulf between one cell and the next – they act as microscopic resistors, slowing down the passage of the impulse while a neurotransmitter is secreted.

Now, imagine a new impression reaching the brain – say yet another telephone number. The impression 'reverberates', linking a number of neurons together into a circuit or engram and this stores the impression as a memory. The neurons in this freshly created circuit are, of course, separated by synapses, each of which puts up a certain amount of resistance to the passage of the impulse from one neuron to the next. And, unless this resistance is broken down, the neurons in this circuit will quickly revert to acting as single nerve cells rather than as part of an engram. This is what happens when the phone number is left in the short term memory. However, as we've seen, by repeating the number it will be consolidated into the long term memory. What this repetition is actually doing is breaking down the synaptic resistance and making it easier for the message to pass between the cells in the engram. As Donald Hebb observed, with repeated use of this memory, the resistance gets smaller and smaller, cementing the memory even more strongly into place. The next question is: how is resistance in the synapses broken down?

Strengthening the links

Again, there are only theories to answer this question rather than established facts. Each theory has its merits, though, and one or more of them may be true. One idea, for example, suggests that with repeated use each neuron in the circuit synthesizes and secretes more of the particular neurotransmitter required for relaying the impulse from one cell to the next. Another theory has it that the synaptic gulf between each cell is narrowed, making the transmission of the impulse more effective. A third comes up with the idea that with repeated use, new axons and dendrites are created to knit the cells in the circuit together more firmly.

The probability that at least one of these processes takes place has been confirmed by a remarkable experiment. Taking lateral thinking to its extremes, this experiment actually measures the level of protein produced by the formation of an engram during the learning process. The basis of the experiment lies in the fact that the neurons and neurotransmitters of the engram are made primarily from two substances – proteins and lipids (fats). As we've seen, it's likely that the learning process – that is, the storing of an impression in the brain as an engram and the breaking down of the synaptic resistance – requires the creation of additional protein-based structures. According to the theories we've just seen, these take the form either of extra neurotransmitters, axons and dendrites, or membrane walls. As learning occurs, therefore, it should be possible to measure the additional building activity taking place in the brain as it forms an engram.

The main challenge in achieving this goal comes from working out a way of recording the protein consumption. Scientists have met this challenge with the help of some simple tools, namely amino acids (the building blocks of protein) labelled with radioactive markers. By following the markers as a radar operator might follow a plane, it should be possible to detect where protein is being built.

The next stage of the experiment involves injecting these amino acids into two groups of laboratory mice. The first group is subsequently allowed to languish in a cage feeding lavishly from trays of food made readily available. The other group, however, is forced to work for its food. This means learning how to use a pulley system methodically to raise a ladder to an elevated platform on which the tray of food sits. As you can see, the first group has no incentive for learning, while for the second group learning is a matter of life and death. In this experiment, the first group is used as a control, to compare the brain consumption of the radioactive aminos with those of the second group.

Once the second group of mice have learned how to obtain their food – and new engrams have supposedly formed in the brain to assist with the learning process – the two sets of mice are X-rayed. While the first group shows no discernible use of the aminos in their brains, the second group shows considerable protein growth in those area where the engrams are expected to be stored – the temporal lobes. This protein consumption has been directly proportionate to the level of learning in the second group of mice. The experiment proves conclusively that protein is used as part of the learning process and that, by extension, physical changes occur in the brain when memories are stored.

Genetic memory?

Another experiment with animals, in this case chicks, has shown that, as they are called upon to learn – that is, store memories, then recall these memories as aids in reacting to new circumstances – there is a resulting increase in the amount of an enzyme called RNA polymerase circulating in their brains. This substance is responsible for creating RNA, one of the two genetic codings of the body. When we store our memories, it seems that RNA is created to assist the process. But what does it do? RNA's function throughout the body is to replicate plans of specific, localized areas of the body from DNA, the body's master blueprint. If the body is short of a muscle cell, for example, a blank strip of RNA will attach itself to the relevant section of DNA and, by moulding itself around that section, create a perfect replica. It will then break off from the DNA and, as a blueprint for that particular muscle cell, bring together the necessary components for building it.

It may be that, whenever we store a memory, RNA is called upon to provide the blueprint of an engram. If so, then it is possible that RNA is responsible for the 'reverberations' we have spoken of. DNA and RNA already provide the body's genetic memory. Could it be that they also provide us with the basis for a conscious one, too? If so, then this in turn begs other questions. Supposing DNA and RNA could store memories – particularly those which by force of repetition had become almost instinctive – could these memories then be passed in the genetic code from one generation to the next? Might we be born with dim, fragmentary recollections of our ancestors' lives? And might this be the source of what we know as déjà vu – the sense of having experienced something before even though we have no recollection of having done so?

Fanciful? Probably, but it is worth mentioning yet another fascinating experiment involving memory and the much put-upon laboratory animals. This involved a trayful of flatworms – pretty unpromising material, you might think. The tray was hooked up to a battery then placed in a dark cupboard. Every time the cupboard was opened and light flooded in, the battery was switched on and the worms given a jolt of electricity, causing them to curl up into tight balls. After continuing this procedure for a week, the battery was removed. However, the worms continued to curl up when exposed to light – their behaviour having been modified by the electric shocks. In the simple mechanisms of their brains, what passed as memory had told them that light preceded pain. This wasn't the last of their troubles. They were then ground up and the slurry fed to a second group of worms. Prior to eating the slurry, this group had demonstrated no adverse signs when exposed to light. However, after their feast, removing them from the cupboard caused them to curl up in exactly the same way as the first group.

It is tempting to say that the second group of worms actually digested and absorbed the first group's memories. What is more likely to have happened is that the levels of neurotransmitters created in the first group's simple brains in response to the shock-and-light conditioning were so high that it caused the second group to react in the same way when it ingested them. All the same, the idea of inheriting grandmother's memory of Zeppelins over London is a lot more intriguing than inheriting her blue eyes. This is very much in the realms of theoretical biochemistry and we are not going to walk any further down this particular path. What is certain is that RNA is important for the memory process and we'll return to the subject in chapter 4.

A conversation piece

Up to now, we've tended to use highly mechanistic terms to describe the processes through which the brain stores memories. We've compared the transformation of stimuli into nerve impulses with the digital encodement of a compact disc; we've spoken of the polyunsaturate-enriched nerves as tuning forks; and engrams as silicon chips. Although using comparisons like these is useful for helping to understand complicated processes, there is a danger that we'll start thinking of the brain as no more than a sort of machine – a computer perhaps. Some behaviourists might argue that this is exactly what the brain is. Other psychologists, though, might say that the crucial factor that separates the brain from simple calculating instruments is a soul. Now the question of whether we possess a soul is one that we cannot answer. Nonetheless, the brain does differ from a computer in other important ways. Let's see how.

During the fifty-year development of the computer, scientists long expected that the main difference between it and the brain would always be that the brain was able to store more information. However, with the advent of supercomputers, silicon chips and sixth generation computing, it has become possible to match the brain's storage capacity with a computer's, neuron for byte (admittedly, a computer with the equivalent storage ability takes up roomfuls of space compared to the 1500cc or so of the brain). However, scientists are now encountering a previously unforeseen but probably unassailable difference between the two. And this difference is semantics.

In its narrowest sense, semantics is the way we put language together from individual words in order to convey information. In a perfect world, language is constructed according to tightly-defined rules. Ideally, subject, verb and object, modifying adverbs, adjectives, pronouns, transitive and passive verbs and prepositions should all fit together in a clear, limpid, unambiguous way. In reality, language – whether spoken or written – is a chaotic, fluid, ever-changing phenomenon in which more rules are broken than obeyed. Consequently, much of the information we obtain from written and spoken language is not gleaned from the way the words themselves are linked together, but from the meaning which we think lies behind them. Sometimes this can lead to terrific confusion. More often than not, though, we effortlessly understand conversation and text even when the meaning is buried in a forest of split infinitives, malapropisms, repetition, self-contradiction, misspelling, bad syntax and tangential interruptions.

However, for a computer to understand language, the meaning has to be set in stone. There can be no room for ambiguity since it is incapable of making inferences – of understanding an intended message even if the message isn't strictly contained in the language. For example, when we are told of a man who has decided to 'circumcise the world', we can infer that he is in fact going to circumnavigate it. To the computer, though, this simply makes no sense. As language is an organic, malleable, above all ambiguous, force, a computer will never be able to master it entirely. The only way it might conceivably happen would be if language as we know it shifted to the colourless, ossified, shrinking language envisaged by George Orwell in his book *1984*. Even then a computer could not match the brain, for, in its broader sense, semantics extends far beyond the ability to perceive meaning within the ambiguity of language. This is because to understand almost everything around us means applying this same semantic flexibility. What exactly does this mean?

Perception from fluidity

For our example, we'll use the letter 'm' although it could just as easily be a colour or face, sound or taste. Every day we encounter this letter in many separate guises. We might see it stamped boldly on a car registration number plate, printed in a looping, classical typeface on a menu, sprayed as graffiti onto a wall or scribbled to us in a hand-written letter. In each case, 'm' – as with all letters of the alphabet – will be recognized instantly, even though we may not have seen it before in that colour, that size, that typeface or that scribble. When we register this letter, it is because we recognize its general shape rather than the specific example.

Arthur Koestler, the novelist and one of this century's most compelling writers of science, once said that a 'large proportion of our memories resemble dregs in a wineglass'. What he meant by this is that, as memory is stored, the specific elements of that memory are gradually stripped away to leave its essence. He used the example of a play in which the exact words spoken fade from our memories within seconds, the meaning of what one character says to another fades within hours and the sequence of scenes and acts within days to leave us with the knowledge that the play was about a homicidal king with a hump. None the less, storing only this barest of essentials in our conscious memories is enough to ensure that, if we saw the play again, even in a different production with different actors, sets and costumes, we would recognize it immediately.

This abstractive memory, as Koestler called it, is the factor that allows us to recognize the different sorts of 'm'. It applies to everything we encounter in life. With it we can recognize different shades of the same colour, the same face at different stages of ageing, and indeed the meaning of what a friend is saying to us when it is buried under an avalanche of badly expressed – or alternatively, poetically expressed –

language. The alternative to this wonderful flexibility is the stereotyped behaviour of the computer – a world without beauty and ugliness, light and shade, lyricism and art. And this is really no alternative at all.

3

Losing your Memory

The first two chapters have shown – if any evidence were needed – what an astonishingly complex and able organ the brain is, as well as illustrating the overwhelming importance of its offspring, memory. We have seen nerve impulses constantly arriving from the farthest reaches of the body, carrying their encoded translations of thousands of separate pieces of information trawled from contacts with the outside world. As they reach the brain they have created 'reverberations', forging custom-built neural networks from among the fifteen-billion-plus-strong agglomeration of neurons. These networks – or engrams – have remained in place often long after the stimuli which caused their creation has faded. At first, the links between the neurons which form these networks are very weak. They can be broken apart by stimuli which interrupt the physical linking of the cells by causing the creation of competing engrams. Through repeated use, though, the bonds have become stronger and in doing so an initial, transient, short term memory has been consolidated through repeated use into a long term memory.

Then, on top of this, we've seen how the brain not only records information in this way, but uses it as the tool with which it learns. By drawing on the available information stored in its memory, the brain is actually able to make inferences – to produce a response that is, in effect, greater than the sum of its memories. Recognizing someone by the back of their head when we've only previously seen their faces, for example, recognizing a composer by a piece of music which we've never heard before, or deciphering the most seemingly illegible of scribbles in a friend's handwritten letter. Each of these demonstrate our ability to expand upon what we know – to learn.

Memory, therefore, isn't only a functional response or a mechanical reflex device. It is our most profound gift and ability. Thanks to its capability of recognizing messages within the most confusing and incomplete data, of drawing conclusions from information a computer would disregard because of its woeful incompleteness, the brain enables us to take the most gigantic imaginative leaps. In this way we play with, and distort, the meaning of language by creating metaphors and, in doing so, give birth to poetry; we abstract certain elements of light and colour from what we see around us, creating the most vivid paintings; we write melodramas by stripping away the super-fluity of life to unearth a tragic, unifying cord that we all recognize. And in each case our understanding and perception of the world around us is enhanced.

Equally, the wonders of science owe their seemingly purpose-ful advances to irrational leaps in the dark. Great scientific breakthroughs have only ever been made by men and women making imaginative suppositions that exceed the available data. And irrespective of what the great figures of science would like us to believe, the respectability of statistical proof has only ever been gathered to prove that initial inspiration.

So take a bow, memory. You tell us how to cross a road, how to walk, how to use a knife and fork, how to recognize people and understand what they are saying. You also help us to extend the farthest limits of our achievements, ennobling us with the spirit of discovery. Imagine what the world would be like with-out you....

How we lose our memory

Despite these wonderful powers, we take our memories for granted. Memory is not a tangible asset such as a car or house that we are conscious of using daily. Nor is it like our sight or hearing. As long as it is there we don't notice it, and perhaps that is the best way for it to be. Because consider how unsettling it can be when it doesn't perform for us as it should. Think, for instance of the irritation, the tantalizing just-on-the-tip-of-my-tongue frustration of a name that eludes you. On occasion we've all experienced a sense of discomfort at not being able to remember, accompanied perhaps by a fleeting shadow of anxiety or anger. In fact, this is itself a trigger for the brain to continue searching subconsciously for the memory when we've given up trying, so that without warning, and when the need for that memory has passed, it pops unannounced into the brain.

Victims of memory loss, though, experience this sense of torment constantly. Rather than a minor irritant, it is a fixed part of their lives, a mental itch they can never scratch. We've all forgotten where we put our keys or cheque book from time to time, but think how dispiriting it would be if we did it day in and day out. And what of the effects on friends and relations if, seconds after making an observation or cracking a joke, you have forgotten doing so and repeat yourself not once but time and time and time again.

'We can be talking quite naturally between ourselves – of little incidents that happened when I was a girl, of going to the science museum as a family, of a little cat we once had – and I'm almost lulled into thinking that everything is OK. Then you catch sight of his eyes and they're just sort of glazed over and he looks confused or stunned as if he's just woken up and he doesn't remember where he is. And I realize that he's probably already forgotten the conversation we just had.' So says Joy of her father, Joseph. Last year, Joseph suffered a stroke. A clot in his brain stopped the blood from reaching parts of his temporal lobes to replenish them with oxygen and food. The neurons in those areas died and, as a result, Joseph became a chronic amnesic. Although some memory has returned – particularly of his long term past – it is almost impossible for him to remember any new experiences. Perhaps the most tragic part of this, though, is that Joseph is acutely aware of his problem.

'I used to be the one that everybody would come to if they wanted to know some obscure piece of general knowledge,' he says. 'I used to have a terrific memory. Now I don't know what day it is or even what year.'

'The worst thing about it,' continues Joy, 'is that although he recognizes and loves me as his daughter, I'm at a fixed historical point for him. He thinks of me with those feelings he had before this stroke. If I were to dye my hair, wear heavy make-up and a different wardrobe of clothes he wouldn't be able to recognize me because I'd have gone outside the rigid view he has of me.

It stops our relationship from developing and I think that's tragic.'

Since Joseph has access to acute recollections of his past, his case is different from that of the classic amnesic we saw in Chapter 1. It also differs enormously from Avril's experiences. Avril's recent fiftieth birthday celebrations were a sombre affair as shortly before, specialists had diagnosed her as suffering from Alzheimer's disease. She had at first attributed her forgetfulness and inability to make decisions to the natural slowing down of middle age but as her memory slip became more pronounced, the symptoms became incontrovertible. 'Twice now I've walked to the shops, got halfway, then had to stop in a panic because I don't know what I'm doing or where I'm going. Sometimes I can't remember the names of my son and daughter-in-law, I regularly forget what to do next when I'm in the middle of doing something simple like making a cup of tea. I was writing out a shopping list the other day. I thought, 'this list is long', read it back and found I'd written the same items two or three times. It really scares me. It makes me feel uncertain of myself and very lonely, especially when I think what is to become of me.'

As you can see, memory loss has many different causes, takes many forms and has differing degrees of severity. Let's look at them one by one.

Forgetfulness by choice

At one level, memory loss arises not out of any physical disability at all, but from an unconscious desire to make our lives more bearable. Sigmund Freud, the father of modern psychoanalysis, who recognized this tendency, classified it in two divisions, straightforward forgetfulness and false recollection. The forgetfulness, he said, often had as its source some unpleasant experience in the patient's past. For example, a young lady called Janet may have once had a heart-breaking affair with a young man called Tony. Years later at a party she is introduced to a friend's husband. A little later she finds herself alone with him. Try as she may she simply can't remember his name – despite being very good at remembering. It is only when she arrives home that she realizes with a shock that he was called Tony. As soon as he had been introduced, her subconscious had flushed the name

straight out of her conscious memory to prevent it from triggering recollections of that other Tony from her past. It is
surprising how common this experience is.

Unlike such forgetfulness, false recollection substitutes one
word, or action, or face, or name for the one we mean to use.
This may have many causes. We may subconsciously dislike the
real one. Alternatively the substitute may more truthfully convey
our feelings. A classic example is the way in which memories of
our childhood years always seem perpetually sunlit when, no
doubt, they were as damp and grey as at any time of life. This
sort of inadvertent substitution also dots our communication
with others. There must be more than one man who, when talk
ing with an attractive and desirable woman about a landmark of
San Francisco, has called it the coitus tower when he meant the
coit tower. And what are we to understand from Margaret
Thatcher when she says: 'We are a grandmother'?

These mistakes are called Freudian slips, a state where the
unconscious reveals itself from behind the studiously maintained
mask of our conscious selves. They might be categorized simply
as absent-mindedness but far from states to be feared, we should
be sensitive to them when they arise since they provide telling
insights into aspects of our personality which are generally
hidden.

The forgetfulness of confusion

A second form of forgetfulness stems from certain necessary limitations of our memories, limitations imposed by the very mechanisms that provide the memory's phenomenal scope and flexibility. This has less to do with forgetfulness than an occasional
inability to recognize or distinguish certain stimuli. Our ability to
make inferences and draw conclusions from what a computer
would treat as incomplete information is due to two related abilities within the brain; firstly the tendency to strip down, or
streamline, memories to their bare essentials (remembering, for
example, only the plot of a play rather than the dialogue); sec-
ondly the cross-referencing of memories thanks to numerous
associations (such as sea and sand, or sea and river). These two
functions interrelate so that, as with the example of Oliver in
Chapter 1 where a fleeting sight of the sea gives rise to a rich

tapestry of memories, we build up a complex picture of the world around us and our place in it.

However, it is this extensive interrelation, coupled with the extreme simplification procedure, that causes the problems. For example, ask a cross-section of people to name a beetle and some would say Colorado, some John Lennon and some Volkswagen. This is a case when the information was simply too vague to infer something from it. Yet in everyday life such vagueness abounds. When a person standing opposite you, for example, says you have a strand of cotton on your left ear, does he mean his left or yours? In most circumstances these occurrences are at worst minor irritants. But imagine what would happen if they took place in environments where safety is a critical factor – such as the control tower of an airport. This is why procedures have been introduced which bypass any possibility of such confusion.

The food of memory

The examples of memory loss that we've just looked at are unavoidable with such a complex network of messages passing between us. However, scientists are starting to realize that a serious physical cause of memory loss stems from problems which are only too avoidable – problems of nutritional deficiency. In fact, there is growing evidence to suggest that memory problems traditionally associated as natural by-products of ageing can be actively fought and prevented with a regime of healthy eating.

The term 'nutritional deficiency' does not mean malnutrition. Rather than not eating enough food, it means that not enough of the right kind of food is eaten. Nowadays, any suggestion in our food-rich society that it is possible to suffer from nutritional deficiencies is treated by most food and medical authorities with surprise if not outright scorn. The average diet, they say, is rich in protein for growth, carbohydrate for energy and loaded with trace elements and minerals for enzymes and co-factors. The shelves of our supermarkets creak under a gigantic range of products. How could deficiency possibly arise in such an environment? Let's find out, and at the same time see how it may affect our memories.

Firstly, when talking about nutrition, it's useful to remember an old nursery rhyme:

For want of a nail, the shoe was lost
For want of a shoe, the horse was lost
For want of a horse, the rider was lost
For want of a rider, the battle was lost
For want of a battle, the kingdom was lost
And all for want of a horseshoe nail.

In this poem, the loss of a single object, seemingly minute and unimportant, causes a chain reaction that escalates catastrophically out of control. In the same way, a shortfall of only one or two nutrients in your diet will reverberate through the entire body. This is because each nutrient is inextricably linked in a biological cycle of creation to all the others. This cycle, called the metabolic pathways, takes in the proteins, minerals, vitamins and fats and, by forging them together in almost infinite variations, creates all the separate structures and chemicals the body needs for living – cell membranes, enzymes, neurotransmitters, bone, muscle and blood to name but a few.

If only one or two chemicals are prevented from entering this cycle, important functions will be unable to occur, in turn stopping others from taking place. If prolonged, the entire process will collapse like a molecular house of cards, with illness and debility following in its wake. Let's see what this means in practice.

The mineral antagonists

Minerals are elements which are used in a mass of bodily reactions – from creating enzymes, generating electrical impulses and maintaining the body's water balance, to crystallizing in the bones and providing the energy we need for life. Unlike the other main food groups – such as proteins – they cannot be made from other substances and must be obtained whole from the soil. Man's mineral supplies are obtained from plants grown in mineral-rich soil and from animals which have grazed on grass growing in the soil.

In the West, farmers wishing to make full use of this soil fertilize it with substances derived from the minerals phosphorus and nitrogen. While the fruit and vegetables grow rapidly as a result, they suffer from other, adverse, effects. Minerals live together in a precarious co-existence. Too much of one mineral causes the levels of others to drop. This is known as antagonism and, when the crops are fed larger amounts of phosphorus and nitrogen, the levels of other minerals such as calcium, magnesium, potassium and zinc are forced to drop.

At the same time, the soil itself, made increasingly acidic by acid rain, also prevents the plants from adequately absorbing important minerals – particularly iron and magnesium. Finally, prior to reaching supermarket displays, the plants are spray-cleaned with a chelating agent, a chemical which, in order to give the plants a lustrous, shiny surface, strips it of those nutritionally important, but aesthetically unpleasing, minerals which make it look duller and greyer.

So what does this disruption of the mineral balance mean for memory? Firstly, it may well disrupt the transmission of impulses along the nerve fibres. As we've seen, the passage of the impulse from one nerve to the next takes place thanks to the body's neurotransmitters bridging the synaptic gulf. The passage of the impulses across the cell, though, is caused by sodium which circulates in the fluid surrounding the cell, and potassium which is found in the fluid inside. As these two minerals have similar electrical charges, they act like the same magnetic poles, that is, they tend to repel each other. This maintains an electrical neutrality between the inside and outside of cells. When the message reaches the cell from a neighbour, sodium is forced across the membrane into potassium's domain within the cell. This depolarizes, or unbalances, the equilibrium of the two elements, causing the cell to discharge a burst of electrcity. The electricity travels the length of the cell until it reaches the necessary axon jutting out into the synaptic gulf where it triggers the secretion of neurotransmitter, and so on to the brain.

However, if our bodies contain a higher than ideal ratio of sodium to potassium – either through too much dietary sodium or too little potassium – then it seems that messages may well be disrupted by biochemical static. Calcium, too, is recognized as an important memory component. Gary Lynch and Michael Baudry, two neurobiologists at the University of California, have recently discovered that calcium is instrumental in causing the physical change that establishes the neural network, or engram, of memory. They found that a calcium-activated enzyme called calpain eats away at certain parts of a neuron's dendrite (the cell's receiving structure on the far side of the synapse from the axon). This allows stores of a special receptor chemical buried deep in the dendrite to flood into the synapse, increasing the cell's sensitivity to incoming neurotransmitters. This in turn forges closer links between the cells and strengthens their ability to form a stable, long-term memory. A shortfall of calcium, therefore, will impair this engram–strengthening tendency.

Calcium metabolism in the body cannot simply be increased by eating foods such as milk and cheese which are rich in the mineral. Metabolism depends on a number of factors, including the presence of adequate magnesium, potassium and vitamin D, each of which are vulnerable to depletion.

Finally, zinc is another chemical which is important for memory formation since it helps to form an enzyme called DNA-dependent RNA polymerase. You may remember that it is this enzyme which bonds a blank strand of the ribosome, RNA, to its parent chromosome, DNA, in order to mould a localized molecular blueprint. Since RNA helps form the memory-storing engrams, zinc is highly important. Yet it is one of the most easily lost minerals in the body. It can be antagonized by fertilizers, by copper (a common mineral in many foods), by cigarette smoke and alcohol. And a man loses almost the entire recommended daily amount of zinc each time he ejaculates – perhaps sex really does make your memory go.

Fat-headedness

Another major cause of deficiency stems from the fats which we ingest. As we say in Chapter 1, essential polyunsaturates are indispensable both in translating experiences into electrical impulses and then relaying them to the brain. They form the membranes of those cells which line our sensory organs (the biochemical tuning forks) and make up various important neurotransmitters (such as acetylcholine). They do this not as individual molecules but in combinations of two fatty acids and a phosphate – forming molecular tridents called phosphatides. It is differing varieties of phosphatide that carry out this most biochemically sensitive work.

The sources of these essential polyunsaturates are oils such as sunflower, safflower, evening primrose and juniper berry for one family known as omega 6 linoleic acids, and fresh fish – meat and oils – and flax seed for the other called omega 3 linolenic acids. Most oil producers claim on their packaging that oils and margarines are high in essential polyunsaturates but this is highly misleading. For the industrial processes which yield these oils – the massive batch pressings to squeeze every last drop from sunflower seeds, for example, as well as the high-pressure bubbling of hydrogen into the oil to turn it into margarine – tend to destroy the nutritional value of the polyunsaturates. Don't forget that to perform the roles they do in the body they must be extraordinarily sensitive to chemical change. If they react in the body to the smallest, slightest stimulus, just think how they react when subjected to these gross manufacturing processes.

The result is that large numbers of these molecules are twisted into nutritionally useless mutations called trans fatty acids. Once in the body they act as biochemical impostors. They masquerade as essential polyunsaturated fatty acids, slotting into the same membranes and neurotransmitter sacs, but unable to perform any of the crucial impulse-carrying tasks when called upon to do so.

Fat and strokes

Essential polyunsaturates also play important roles in regulating the levels of saturated fats (more inert and inactive than the unsaturates) and cholesterol in the blood. A loss of the polyunsaturates, therefore, may cause the blood to become sticky and sludgelike as, untended, these other fats agglomerate harmfully. Blood pressure will start to rise, the arteries harden and in time blood clots may ocur. If this happens in the brain, then one of the results may be what doctors call an infarction and what we call a stroke. Single or multi infarctions are responsible for a fifth of all cases of dementia. They are caused, as in the case of Joseph which we looked at earlier, by the blood being prevented from reaching some areas of the brain, causing the neurons to die off and in turn leading to amnesia.

Aminos and memories

Another contributory nutritional factor towards arteriosclerosis, plaque formation and an eventual stroke can be traced to a short-fall of amino acids – the molecular building blocks of protein. Although we eat more than enough protein in terms of quantity, the quality is not always good enough. Even supposing we ingest high quality protein, rich in essential amino acids, there simply may not be enough vitamins and minerals to create the co-factors needed to break the protein up into its constituent aminos prior to being re-created in the body.

A perfect example is the effects on plaque formation and memory of an enzyme called glutathione synthase. As part of a multi-stage metabolic pathway of an amino called methionine, one of the intermediate amino acids is a substance called homo-cysteine. Homocysteine has abrasive qualities and can scar sur-rounding tissue very easily, leading to the build-up of plaque. Luckily, the enzyme glutathione synthase and vitamin B_6 com-bine the amino acid serine with homocysteine to produce a harmless amino acid called cystathione. In a healthy body, this process takes place almost instantaneously and the potential dan-ger is averted.

Sometimes, though, thanks to nutritional deficiency, or habits such as smoking and drinking heavily, there simply isn't enough of the enzyme glutathione synthase to convert this abrasive amino. Instead, it will be left to circulate in the arteries, swirling like a metabolic scouring pad in a tumble dryer, scuffing the ves-sel walls and creating convenient deposition points for fatty plaques. Glutathione synthase is created from substances such as the vitamins B_{12} and B_6 (both of which are vulnerable to destruc-tion from overcooking, cigarette smoke and poor digestion), and several minerals.

Another amino acid involved in the memory connection is called arginine. It is the parent molecule of a chemical called spermine which plays an as-yet undetermined role with RNA in the formation of memories. The much-admired American psy-chiatrist, Carl Pfeiffer, found that people with good memories have correspondingly high levels of spermine, while those with poorer memories – and especially those with Alzheimer's disease – have equally low levels. The tendency towards low levels of amino acids is worrying since they also form the backbones of most of the forty or so neurotransmitters so far identified.

Don't panic

Bearing in mind the way in which so many nutritional factors affect memory – either directly such as the result of a decline in essential polyunsaturates in the neurons, or indirectly through the factors which contribute to a stroke – it is likely that deficiencies form one of the most basic causes of memory loss. We saw in Chapter 1 the damage that a virus can do to the brain. Many nutritionalists would even argue that susceptibility to such viruses only occurs when the immune system is itself weakened by nutritional deficiency.

We are not saying that if you are deficient in some of the nutrients we've looked at then you will fall prey to memory loss. However, it is a simple fact that if the products needed to support a particular function are in short supply, then that function will inevitably suffer. The effects of deficiency aren't felt at once. They accumulate over many years. It may be decades before their effects are felt, and that sort of timespan is bound to breed complacency among potential victims. However, isn't it better to insure as best you can against this problem ever arising by taking steps to protect yourself now? In Chapter 5 we'll look at people whose quality of lives have been enhanced by special programmes of high potency nutritional supplementation and show you how to follow similar programmes to boost and protect your own brain power.

Now it is time to turn our attentions to the cause of memory loss that creates more concern than any other – Alzheimer's disease.

The demented epidemic

While strokes are responsible for a fifth of all victims of dementia – the physical and emotional loss of control of which memory loss is a major characteristic – Alzheimer's disease is alone responsible for a staggering half. It is a chronic degenerative disease afflicting 2 per cent of the population over 65 but may start in victims as young as 40. It was first recognized in 1907 by a

German neurobiologist, Aloiz Alzheimer, who defined its symptoms. She described the way it turned bright, lively individuals progressively into disorientated, sometimes aggressive, shadows of themselves, incontinent, unaware of their surroundings and totally dependent on others for their welfare.

The disease itself seems to adopt four distinct stages. The first, as we saw with Avril earlier in the chapter, is a sense in the victim that he or she is 'getting on a bit'. Their activity is less spontaneous, thinking and responding to stimuli take longer. With the second stage, the victim starts forgetting recent events, has difficulty planning for the future and making decisions. Then, with the third stage, their personalities start to change. They become restless and irritable, are easily confused and self-absorbed, and lack any warmth towards friends and relatives. Finally, their personalities seem to disappear altogether. They will wander aimlessly, repeat mumbled phrases time and again, be incapable of the simplest actions.

The disease is irreversible and incurable. Research shows that it is characterized by three physical changes in the brain; atrophy, or wastage, of the brain cells; the formation of abnormally thick bunches of cells called neurofibrillary tangles; and plaques which clog the blood vessels and outer cortex of the brain. it is a frightening catalogue of decline made all the worse by the fact that we have no definite idea of its causes, let alone of how to cure it. There are, however, plenty of theories. Let's take a look at them.

Alzheimer theories

One idea has it that the disease is genetically transmitted. The basis of this concept lies in the fact that both Down's sydrome and thyroid disease have a higher incidence among families of Alzheimer's disease sufferers. Furthermore, almost all those with Down's syndrome who survive to old age develop neurological symptoms identical to Alzheimer's. Another idea suggests that the disease might be caused by a slow-acting virus similar to herpes that takes hold due to a breakdown in the body's immunological defences.

What seems more likely, though, is that in common with other forms of memory loss, Alzheimer's disease has a nutritional source. Frances Abalan, a French neurobiologist, suggests that it is a manifestation of a bodywide deficiency of vital nutrients. For proof he points to the fact that most patients suffer from malnutrition and emaciation, especially in the later stages of the disease. That they are prone to frequent infections also suggests that the immune system receives inadequate nutritional support. Furthermore, in blood tests, Alzheimer patients are commonly shown to have low levels of B vitamins, vitamin C, minerals and amino acids – all of which are vital for the body's metabolic pathways and particularly for healthy brain function.

Other tests on brain tissue show that the degree of memory loss in patients is directly proportionate to the loss of an enzyme called cholinacetyltransferase (CAT for short). This enzyme participates in the formation of acetylcholine, one of the most important neurotransmitters responsible for learning and memory. Acetylcholine is the derivative of a metabolic pathway that starts with a phosphatide called lecithin and continues with another called choline. Researchers have long associated lecithin and choline with memory formation but when they were administered as supplements to Alzheimer patients, their memories showed no improvement at all. This suggested, therefore, that it wasn't the acetylcholine which was in short supply but the chemical which transferred it to the nerve cells – CAT.

So what prevents the body from manufacturing this important enzyme? Like the best detective thriller, the search for clues involves numerous dead ends, pathways which lead back on themselves and others which seem to veer further and further away from the target. However, despite numerous false starts, this last path is being mapped out doggedly by Australian psychiatrist, Dr Chris Reading. He has formulated two theories and, despite the twisting, devious route, he may well be on to something. The first theory is that patients don't have enough CAT because the raw material nutrients are unavailable in the metabolic pathways to create it. This may be caused by inadequate diets or poor quality food. Alternatively, it may have something to do with allergies. In his research, he has found that a high number of Alzheimer patients share allergies to everyday foods such as the proteins in wheat, rye and milk. This allergy leads to an inflamed gut which prevents nutrients from being adequately absorbed. Over the years the problem is compounded massively and leads inexorably to Alzheimer's disease.

If this theory proves to be true, it will serve to link the separate possible causes together into one unifying explanation. It will explain why the disease may be hereditary since allergies definitely can be passed from one generation to the next; it will explain why viruses take hold so easily in Alzheimer patients; and it will account for the depressed levels of nutrients in their blood.

Dr Reading's second theory is that, rather than being unable to absorb food, the allergic inflammation creates a state known as leaky bowel syndrome. This is highly dangerous since toxins which the gut would normally prevent from entering the body are permitted to force their way in. The next question is: what are these toxins and which ones would affect the memory? At this point, the detective's twisting path straightens out and widens into a dimly-lit yard. Stopping short we come face to face with one of the most dangerous villains in the entire story. One which, in recent years has become more closely associated with dementia than any other. Its name? Aluminium.

4

The Metal and the Memory

Until quite recently, medical experts paid very little attention to aluminium. To industrialists, on the other hand, this metallic element was a godsend. The fact that it was light and tensile but at the same time extremely strong made it ideal for thousands of commercial applications. What's more, its natural abundance made it very cheap. As the number of uses grew, it was employed in everything from cooking-foil and pans and containers for takeaway food to car components.

Better still, the little research that was conducted into its effects on human metabolism showed that negligible amounts were absorbed by the body only to be excreted harmlessly in the urine. This made it an ideal food additive. Aluminium phosphate was used as an emulsifier in certain processed cheeses, table salt was adulterated with either sodium silico aluminate or aluminium calcium silicate to prevent it from caking, while potassium alum – an aluminium-based compound – was used as a bleaching agent to create white flour. It was used in coffee whitener and, as aluminium hydroxide, in numerous brand-named antacid preparations. And when applied to the skin researchers also found that it prevented perspiration. Needless to say it quickly became a staple ingredient in antiperspirants and deodorants.

Of course, as far back as the early 1960s, some researchers had attempted to link aluminium with certain neurological disorders but, due to lack of evidence, no one took much notice. Then things began to go wrong.

In 1976, aluminium hit the headlines with a vengeance. While conducting a series of low-key experiments into the pathology of Alzheimer's disease, a team of Canadian researchers turned their attention to the cords of swollen neurofibrillary tangles that characterized the illness. It seemed fairly certain that these tangles were peculiar to senile demented brains and that their effect was literally to tangle the nerve impulses, causing confusion and behavioural problems. The Canadian team was attempting to find out what actually caused these tangles. As they probed deeper they found to their astonishment aluminium deposits of between ten and thirty times greater than that found in the normal brain – not just in one victim of senility but in one after another.

Prompted by this discovery, previously unconnected findings from researchers working around the globe began to accumulate, painting a disturbing picture of the effects of aluminium on brain health. When applied to the brain surface, for example, aluminium was found to trigger electrical activity, leading to seizures or fits. When aluminium was injected into the cranial fluids surrounding the brains of a group of laboratory rabbits, there was a rapid degeneration of brain tissue identical to the effects of Alzheimer's disease. Equally, cats injected with the same proportions of aluminium to that found in Alzheimer patients displayed symptoms of slow learning, disorientation and forgetfulness.

Aluminium was also implicated in dialysis dementia. Here, victims of kidney failure, using dialysis machines to filter impurities from their blood, were suffering certain behavioural abnormalities in alarming numbers. These symptoms were similar to the early and middle stages of Alzheimer's diseases: disorientation, confusion, indecisiveness and amnesia. It was then found that in each case the water used to purify the dialysis patients' blood contained high levels of aluminium. Slowly, the pieces of the jigsaw started to come together, showing that aluminium was not the benign, all-purpose metal that people had supposed. Anything but.

As aluminium research burgeons, scientists are discovering just how widespread are its effects on the body. Once it has been absorbed, it tends to become concentrated in the lungs, liver and along the nerve fibres of the brain. It is especially harmful to neurons as it binds to the DNA, preventing the constant replacement and growth of nerve tissue. As we've seen, DNA is the essential master-plan of the body. When new tissue is required, an RNA replica of the specific part of the body needing renewal is made. Imagine what would happen if, in the process of the physiological changes which occur during the formation of an engram, the DNA responsible for overseeing that change is blocked. Then the neural links will not be forged as they should, the memory will not be consolidated and it will fade. This makes recent memories particularly vulnerable to the effects of aluminium and may explain why it is these that are first affected by Alzheimer's disease. However, even the engrams of well-established, long term memories need renewal and if blocked by aluminium, they too start to disintegrate.

Aluminium has also been found to inhibit the actions of a number of enzymes including cholineacetyltransferase (CAT), hexokinase and beta dopamine transferase. Each of these plays an important role in the creation of neurotransmitters, and blockage may prevent messages being relayed to and from the brain.

Other effects of aluminium include causing an increase in the production of a chemical called parathyroid hormone (PTH). PTH is a hormone whose job is to withdraw calcium from the bones. It is normally only secreted when a shortfall of calcium elsewhere in the body requires dipping into the massive amounts of the mineral stockpiled in the skeleton. However, when there is no such shortage, the action of aluminium in causing PTH to withdraw calcium unnecessarily floods it into the soft tissue of the arteries and cells. Once there, calcium has an excitory effect on the motor neurons – those nerve cells responsible for carrying messages from the brain to the muscle. This can lead to the sort of jerky, uncoordinated movement typical of Parkinson's disease, an illness that scientists are now also partially attributing to aluminium.

Aluminium also acts as a trigger for free radical activity. Free radicals are not a group of itinerant socialists, but molecules in the body which plunder electrons from the atoms of other, neighbouring molecules. In doing so they cause the character of the neighbouring molecules to change. If unchecked, this causes a chain reaction through a network of neighbouring molecules that damages the structure of the organ in which they sit. The best way to picture the effects of this is to imagine that for a split second a swath of brickwork on your house, sweeping diagonally up from door lintel to the corner of the guttering, turns to jelly. Before it turns back to solid brick, the weight of the roof above it, lacking support, starts to collapse. So, even after the brickwork has reassumed its natural state, you are still left with an almighty crack in the wall. Translate this to the sensitive tissue of the brain and you get an idea of the free radical effects triggered by aluminium. Many researchers feel it may be one of the causes both of the neurofibrillary tangles and the widespread atrophy of neurons which characterize Alzheimer's disease.

So how easy is it for us to ingest aluminium? Minute quantities are contained unavoidably in most foods and the body copes with these well enough. However, there are other ways in which we might inadvertently ingest more than we strictly have to. Acid rain, for example, dissolves aluminium out from the soil and flushes it into the water supply. Cooking acidic fruits and vegetables, such as tomatoes or rhubarb, in aluminium pots, or storing them in aluminium containers, dislodges molecules into the food. And, of course, some processed foods still contain aluminium.

If Dr Reading's theories are correct (see page 45) and leaky bowel syndrome is a major contributory factor towards Alzheimer's disease, then people with this problem are at much greater risk from the effects of aluminium than the rest of us. In Chapter 9 we'll see what measures are available both for treating leaky bowel and for eradicating as much aluminium as possible from our diets.

As with other possible health hazards, there are no incontrovertible facts as yet to say that aluminium is a cause of Alzheimer's disease, rather an accumulating mass of circumstantial evidence. Then again, circumstantial evidence was all we had for many years to tell us that smoking is bad for health. Now, definitive research studies link the toxins produced by smoking with medical problems.

5

Memorable Triggers

In future chapters we'll see what can be done to help people whose memories have been permanently impaired by factors such as Alzheimer's disease, inadequate nutrition, stroke and injury. We'll also look at the steps you can take to help ensure that you yourself don't fall victim to chronic memory loss and its accompanying emotional traumas. Before this, though, we are going to address ourselves to those people who, although not suffering from any physical symptoms of brain illnesses, are nevertheless plagued by irritating lapses of memory and absentmindedness. Unless we're very much mistaken, we're referring to almost every single person reading this book. If you forget the name of a familiar face at an embarassing moment, or forget to put the rubbish out for the dustman, have difficulty remembering the plots of books you've enjoyed, or even find it impossible to learn snatches of Shakespeare for impressing your friends at parties, then read on. For in this chapter, we're going to show you some remarkably effective ways of improving your memory power – perhaps even to the extent of boosting your powers of recall to a level you would never have thought possible. There is no arcane secret involved, merely some simple suggestions for utilizing an ability that you already have.

Good memory – we all have it

If you think of yourself as irredeemably absent-minded, the first thing to realize is that, barring actual physiological difficulties (such as Alzheimer's disease) your brain has a capacity for storing more memories than you would accumulate in five lifetimes, let alone one!

If this is true, and it is, then why should anyone have difficulty remembering? After all, it isn't as if there's a shortage of space. The simple answer is that people do not have difficulty remembering. You and I have the potential to observe, store and remember every bit as much information as all but the most phenomenally gifted owners of photographic memories (and who knows, with training we may be able to equal even their abilities). Psychologists now think that a so-called 'bad memory' has nothing whatsoever to do with memory itself (that is, the physical formation of the neuron circuits we call engrams). Instead, it is believed that bad memory is caused by shortcomings in the recall mechanism. This is the function that actually delves into the brain when a memory is required, its job to locate and deliver that memory to the conscious. The recall mechanism works much like a secretary rummaging through the indices on numerous filing cabinets in the office looking for the correct file. If the indices have been sloppily and inaccurately labelled and the files heaped haphazardly into the cabinets, then no matter how important the information contained in those files, the secretary will take a long time to find them. She might never find them. The same is true of the recall mechanism when it searches the brain for a memory.

Whereas the actual formation of the engram (the information in the file) is a sublime biochemical process working quite beyond the range of our control, our ability to influence the way in which memories can be recalled (that is, located in the filing cabinets) is something we can do a lot to change. In essence it means giving new, clear indices to our mental filing cabinets. So how can we do this?

Trigger happy

You may remember in Chapter 1 how we saw that every memory we experience is evoked from our subconscious by its association with a separate, but related, stimulus or memory. We looked at each of the classic triggers. These were events that: occur near each other or at the same time; that are similar or contrast with each other; create a cause and effect; are part and whole; particular and general; or are part of a numerical contiguity. In fact Saint Augustine went even further when he suggested that the only criterion necessary for one idea or event to provide an association with another is that they occurred or were active at the same time, no matter how incompatible.

As a graphic example of the effects of these triggers, we watched the mood of our itinerant software salesman, Oliver, change from one of jubilation to one of profound melancholy. This change was caused by recalling a flood of youthful memories in turn triggered unconsciously by sighting a view that had been part of his turbulent holiday romance. This is just one example of a phenomenon that is constantly bombarding us and modifying our behaviour. Another example of the way that associations trigger memories is a slight but insightful story told by a cook about the door of his fridge. Since this fridge was installed slanting slightly forward of upright, whenever he opened the fridge door it swung around to bang against the cupboard door on the adjacent kitchen unit. Consequently he got into the habit of sticking out his hand to stop and steady the door before it completed its swing. Having consequently had the height of the fridge adjusted so that the door doesn't swing open, he now finds himself still extending his hand as an unconscious reflex to steady the door, even though he now has no reason to. The door's past associations have triggered memories of a certain kind of behaviour.

Triggers like these affect us all the time in every way. Most of them we are either not conscious of or can do nothing about. Subtle triggers such as long-forgotten smells, for example, are renowned for giving rise to poignant memories. On the other hand, in certain ways we use triggers calculatingly and deliberately. An alarm clock is used to remind us that we must fall out of bed at a certain time, an appointments diary that we have to meet certain people on a given day, a flashing light on the dashboard that the time is overdue to put some oil in the car. Our waking and dreaming lives are conducted in a mesh of these triggers, each of which gives rise to a specific set of memories and thus propels us through our lives on an instinctive stream of consciousness.

Triggers, then, are the spark plugs which ignite our memories and, of course, these memories become in turn triggers for others. Some people are amazed by the memories that sometimes pop into their consciousnesses seemingly out of the blue, but once they retrace their previous trains of thought they discover a logical progression of memories – one triggering the next – that leads to the current revelation. The trigger is the key for unlocking the memory. What we are going to do is show you how to use it much more creatively than merely as a diary or an alarm clock. We are going to give you a blueprint for custom-building your triggers to recall whatever memory you please.

Triggers of the absurd

In the early chapters, we delved in considerable depth into the mechanics of memory. We looked at the way in which external stimuli are converted to electrical impulses which are then transmitted to the brain where they form engrams. Towards the end of Chapter 1 we used a sub-heading to which we asked you to pay particular attention and subsequently try to remember. For those of you who've forgotten what the heading was, it was entitled: Compact discs and alchemy. Now that we've reminded you of the heading, can you remember the subject it dealt with? We'll give you a moment to think about it. Why did we use such seemingly incongruous objects for the sub-heading? What have mediaeval science and modern digital technology to do with the brain? You might now recall that they were used as metaphors to simplify, and also hopefully clarify, the transmission mechanisms of the brain. The heading was used very deliberately because since it was out of the ordinary you, the reader, would be more likely to remember it. And, in remembering it, you would use it as a trigger to recall the information to which it related.

The information in question was the way in which the nerve cells lining our sense organs convert external stimuli into electrical impulses in a seemingly alchemical manner; and the way these impulses are then carried along the nerve fibres in digital impulses similar to compact discs. The chances are that there are a good many more of you who are able to remember the explanation of the process when it is couched in colourful language than if it is written in a dry, scientific manner giving only the facts. You would have switched off, and who would blame you?

This gives further, valuable, insight into the nature of triggers. For greatest effectiveness, not only should triggers correspond to one or more of the conditions of association (part and whole, cause or effect and so on), they should also be out of the ordinary. In this way, our initial interest will be engaged more successfully, making subsequent recall that much easier.

For proof of the way that interest in a stimulus aids memory, you only have to look at a schoolboy scolded by his frustrated maths teacher for his seeming inability to grasp the intricacies of arithmetic. No matter how clearly she tries to explain the subject he just doesn't seem to understand. Yet at home, this same boy pores over old editions of Wisden cricket yearbooks memorizing with ease the batting and bowling averages of his past heroes. Then, with a mental dexterity that would amaze his teacher, he calculates how such averages would be affected should a bowler from one era meet a batsman from another. Essentially, his maths lesson and the cricketing daydreams are very similar. They both require a mastery of certain mathematical theories and a clear grasp of figures. Yet the maths lesson is firmly rooted in the abstract: it has no meaning or relevance for the schoolboy. The cricket, on the other hand, holds a romantic fascination for him. It is peopled by elegant, heroic warriors, their achievements recorded like rolls of honour. Because he has an emotional stake, he remembers the cricketing information effortlessly.

If, somehow, the maths lesson could be raised to a similar level of relevance, the boy would have no learning difficulty (and to be fair, modern school curricula are making this leap). As it is, it's likely that rather than forgetting the maths he was taught, the boy never learned it in the first place. His interest was so low that no sooner were the weak engrams formed than his lack of attention allowed other stimuli to break them up. This is an identical process to the experiments we saw in Chapter 2 when volunteers, attempting to memorize phone numbers, were thwarted when they were forced to recite meaningless sequences of numbers in between.

To summarize, then, what we think of as a good memory depends not on the physical ability to form strong engrams in the brain – we can all do that. What it does depend on is the ability to recall the memory stored in that engram by using an evocative trigger, and the desire to store the memory in the first place by finding it suitably interesting. These observations are virtual platitudes – seemingly meaningless because they are so very obvious. Yet they hold the key to improving your memory and subsequently enhancing all aspects of your life. Because, quite simply, all you have to do to remember anything at all – regardless of its complexity – is to create an interesting, evocative trigger. There are a number of ways of doing this. Let's look at them.

Finding the link

Perhaps the most fascinating way of assisting your powers of recall is to use the link method. It is certainly the most absurd and this is why it works so well. The following explanation may seem to describe a process that is so long-winded and involved as to be utterly impractical when attempted in the 'real' world. However, it does work and with practice and patience will pay enormous dividends.

As we've seen, all our memories are recalled by subconscious triggers. The link method involves substituting these unconscious triggers for conscious ones. Rather than explain the theory, we'll show the method in practice. Malcolm is a young man who greatly enjoys reading. He particularly likes encountering new and unfamiliar words, discovering their meaning, then fitting them into his everyday vocabulary. This, he feels, increases his range of self-expression. However, much to his annoyance, he quickly forgets many of these new words almost as soon as he has read them. This, he thinks, is thanks to their unfamiliar sounds.

To overcome the problem, he decides to try the link method on the next new word he finds. Since our memories are primarily visual in nature, the link method works by associating word sounds with colourful, evocative images – in effect making puns out of them. Let's see what this means with Malcolm's next word. The word happens to be 'fastidious' which his dictionary defines as 'difficult to please; discriminating'. Putting aside the last, 'us', syllable of the word, Malcolm concentrates on the first two 'fast' and 'idi'; he then imagines the most absurd visual pun possible. In his mind's eye, he pictures a film of the former Ugandan despot (Idi) speeded up (fast) so that his movements are jerky and erratic. Hence fast-idi. Then, to link the sound to the meaning, he imagines this hyperactive figure attempting to choose a chocolate from a selection on a huge tray he has just been offered but, despite devoting all his concentration to deciding which chocolate appeals, is unable to find one he likes (hence 'difficult to please; discriminating').

By creating this strange picture in his mind, Malcolm has satisfied all the important criteria for better recall; he has created an evocative trigger while at the same time forcing himself to take an interest in the word by giving the meaning a funny and satisfying visual definition. A few hours later, he wonders what that word was. Instantly the picture appears in his mind and the word and its meaning drop into place. With time and repeated use the image fades leaving only the word and its meaning crystal clear in his mind.

This, then, is the basis of the link method and with it you can learn almost anything you choose. And we're not confining it to single words. Many people use the method with phenomenal success to learn long and complicated lists. To show how, let's assemble an arbitrary collection of items from around the house. Run your eyes over the following list as slowly and deliberately as you need, then look away and see how many you can remember:

stapler; watch; key; book; television; curtain; iron; yo-yo; cassette recorder; razor; pillow; painting; typewriter; briefcase; candelabra.

At first you'll probably remember as many as ten or twelve of the items, although not necessarily in the right order. After a while, though, your memory of them will fade. If you try and remember them this time tomorrow, you'll be hard pressed to list five. We're going to show you how to remember them all, in order and for as long as you like.

Again, the method involves making bizarre visual associations – this time between pairs of words: first and second, second and third, third and fourth and so on. Therefore, recalling the second item will trigger the third, the third the fourth and right on through the entire list. We'll show you how. Read the following descriptions slowly and, above all, attentively.

We began with a stapler and a watch so you might imagine a stapler that, when punched, stamps ticking watch faces onto sheafs of paper. Then, to link a watch up with the third word, key, you could picture a watch face with keys in place of hands. Linking key and book you may imagine a book's pages blowing in a breeze with a great hole in the shape of a keyhole cut in each page. To tie the book with television you might visualize hundreds of tiny televisions crammed into bookshelves. For the next word, curtain, you might have a curtain drawing back from the screen of a television as if it were a theatre stage. For iron, you might picture someone holding a huge iron and running it up and down a curtain to flatten out the folds. For yo-yo you could imagine the iron spinning up and down on a long piece of string. For cassette recorder why not imagine two yo-yos in place of the cassette endlessly winding and unwinding a piece of string from one spool to the other. For razor, imagine a man shaving with a cassette recorder – with loud music coming out instead of the razor's buzz. For pillow, imagine trying to cover it with lather and shave it. For painting, picture a classical nude reclining on a bed covered in sumptuous pillows. For typewriter, imagine typing on a painted canvas – of the selfsame nude perhaps – wrapped around the cylinder where the paper usually goes. For briefcase simply imagine carrying a case laden with typewriters, so heavy that you can hardly walk with it. And finally, for candelabra, why not use the image of hundreds of tiny briefcases suspended in a group from the ceiling, each emitting a warm golden glow.

If you are satisfied that you've read and pictured each of these images then carry on.

Later, we'll set you some tasks of your own. When we do, remember that the key to establishing and recalling these words is to find the most arresting possible link for each item. The more absurd the better, but don't spend too long deliberating about each image. The first one to pop into your head is usually the best. If you can, though, try and make the image an active one (the watch hands revolving around the face very quickly, the curtain opening and closing, the revolving iron spinning up and down on the string, are good examples) as this also seems to stir the ability to recall. Finally, picture your objects as much out of proportion as you can, distorting the size of the objects and creating huge numbers of them.

Once you've worked out a link for each word or item you have to recall, you'll find that you can recall them with relative ease by working through the associations. Of course, to begin with, this will seem a rather complicated and time-consuming method of memorizing the words. With regular practice, though, you'll soon become adept at memorizing, then recalling at will, incredibly long lists of objects that you would have never thought possible. And one of its joys is that it's a skill that you can practise at any time. When standing in a supermarket or bus queue, pick out a handful of objects, conceive the visual associations, then see how successfully your recall of them is triggered later in the day.

You may be wondering what the possible use of such a method is, beyond its appeal as a party trick. The answer is that this method can be used whenever, wherever and for whatever you choose. Working out your shopping list is one obvious example. Or at work, you might have a series of jobs to do, phone calls to make, memos to send, meetings to attend, deliveries to see to. Of course, some people might prefer to keep a note of these things with a diary and memo pad. Fair enough, except while diaries can be mislaid, an active memory cannot and if you hone your recall ability it will be that much sharper in situations where you have no choice but to depend on your memory.

What sort of situations would those be? What about where an executive is called upon to give a business presentation to his or her board, or a group of prospective clients? Here, reading from notes prevents the executive from establishing the important eye contact and robs what he says of spontaneity. Such business people who successfully use the link method write out their presentations fully in advance then read through them, highlighting the key points. These points can then be used as triggers to recall the rest of the text so that all the executive need do is learn them. The same can be used in a classroom environment where a tutor is delivering a lecture to his or her pupils.

It can also be applied when it comes to giving a speech – in a debate perhaps, or at an after-dinner function, or in the graveyard of would-be orators, the wedding reception. The amount of time, effort and expense involved in arranging a wedding, after all, is phenomenal. Yet, more often than not, wedding speeches are an embarrassment of halting sentences, misread notes or perfunctory and incoherent mumbles. Much better, surely, to spend half an hour reviewing what's to be said, writing it down if need be, then establishing a series of triggers to bring what you want to say sharply and clearly into focus at that moment when you have to stand up to give the speech.

Another area where a lack of concentration and focus can lead to terrific embarrassment when the memory fails is in forgetting names and faces. This sort of absentmindedness must be one of the most irksome – and possibly hurtful – varieties of all. No matter, the link method is wonderfully effective in helping you to remember names and faces – and, what's more, relate the one to the other. As with the example of Malcolm's word (what was it?) it involves creating images from the constituent sounds of a person's name and then relating it to a prominent facial characteristic.

Generally, surnames fall into one of three categories:

1 names that you can associate in your mind's eye with a well-known namesake such as Redford, Reagan and Hemingway;

2 names that automatically conjure up a picture either due to their links with working professions – such as Carpenter, Cook or Smith – or simply trigger strong visual associations because of their meanings as words – such as Coley, Ash or Hastie;

3 names that have few, if any, associations. This is by far the biggest group, ranging from Abercrombie to Zychowicz and passing in between through such luminaries as Ibbotson, Marszalek, Raybone and Vadgoma. (All chosen at random from a local telephone directory.)

So, how do we remember such names? Let's start with an easy example, a real-life acquaintance by the name of Bernhard Cook. Bernhard immediately suggests 'burn hard' and, together with the surname, conjures up the picture of a cook zealously over-cooking something in a frying pan, his face lit up hellishly by the flames from the gas ring. However, if you were introduced to him for the first time, such an image might lodge the name in your mind but how could you link this to his face? Simple, you pick the prominent facial characteristic and incorporate it into your mental image – and don't forget, the absurder, the better. In Bernhard's case he has a large, rather unsightly mole on his forehead. All you have to do is imagine the mad cook frying the mole in his frying pan. Disgusting? Good, because you won't be likely to forget it. Imagine you've been introduced to Bernhard at a party. You speak for a bit then drift apart. Later, the two of you happen to meet up again and it's clear he can't remember your name. Neither can you recall his. Instantly, however, the sight of the mole triggers the mental image and, hey presto, up pops his name. 'Hello Bernhard,' you say, 'enjoying yourself?' Immediately the man experiences an innocent mixture of flattery at being remembered so effortlessly and contrition at having forgotten your name. You have him, as they say, at a disadvantage. This book isn't about learning to play power games with people, but the potential for such a system in helping to assert yourself in company is very clear.

OK, what about something a little more difficult? Let's try one of the aforementioned names from the telephone directory, Mr Zychowicz – pronounced 'sickovitch'. At the risk of becoming too unsavoury, the image that immediately comes to mind is of a witch (vitch), dressed in black tattered rags, a broomstick by her side, vomiting (sicko). Unpleasant it may be but it's impossible to deny the visual force of the image. What the gentleman actually looks like is anyone's guess so let's assume he has a mop of shocking blond hair, as straight and white as bleached straw, and incorporate that into the picture of our poor, retching witch. She might be kneeling on some straw, for example, she might even have hair like that herself, her broomstick might have a straw brush. The visual link with the subject's name is very important since, without it, you might begin to confuse one name with another's appearance. Knowing Bernhard, he wouldn't be too pleased to be greeted as Mr Zychowicz.

Now, to see how much you've learnt, overleaf are the pictures of ten characters together with their names. See if you can use the link method to learn their names while at the same time recognizing their faces through some distinctive physical characteristic.

Putting it down on paper

So far we've hardly mentioned at all the importance of writing things down in helping you to remember. A lot of research has been conducted into the way writing helps to reinforce one's memories, and there can be little doubt that it can play a major role. It is much easier to remember something when you take the trouble to make a response, and writing is one of the most obvious ways of doing so. However, very often, people write something down in hope that it will help them remember, without

Jamie
Nielson

Henry
Shires

Julie
MacDougall

Geoff
Bick

Sarah
Sheehan

Fraser
Cheney

Sally
Mooney

David
Walkind

Alison
Anderson

Miriam
Swanston

really taking in what it is they're writing. This response is as passive as neglecting to focus on someone's name when he or she is introduced. For there to be any realistic hope of remembering, whatever is written must be an active part of that process.

Writing without recall is a typical response among schoolchildren when writing about a subject which holds little interest for them. If a teacher dictates some course work to a pupil who finds the course dull and uninteresting, the pupil's response will be mechanically instinctive – forgetting as soon as it has been written down, rather than remembering once it has been written. A similar response happens with secretaries who, when forced to type repetitive reports and memos all day, often lose sight of the meaning of what it is they are writing. This can lead to some elementary and horrendous mistakes in meaning.

On the other hand, writing will actively help you to remember if you have an emotional stake or interest in whatever it is you are trying to learn. If, for example, when abroad you hear a foreign word whose sound and meaning you are unfamiliar with, writing the word down in a vocabulary book once you have looked it up in a dictionary will consolidate its meaning – especially if you also use the link method to evoke a stimulating mental image of the word. The best way of writing to remember, therefore, is to use it as a means of working out a systematic list of trigger words that can then be learnt by the link method.

Abbreviated learning

Another popular way of improving recall is to use mnemonics. This procedure involves essentially removing the first letter from each word on an established list of words, then either putting these letters together to form a single word or using them as the first letters of different words to form a memorable epigram. Most people, for example, have heard of the saying 'Every Good Boy Deserves Favour' to remember the notes that are on the lines of a musical stave in the treble clef. The weakness with mnemonics is that while they can be used with considerable success for particular lists – such as all the invertebrate phylums, the components of the eye, the eight essential amino acids, and so on – you couldn't be expected to use it to remember an *ad hoc* list. The link method, in contrast, is much more flexible.

In Chapter 6 we'll see the memory techniques in practice. Before going on, though, let's see how many of the words you can remember from the list we looked at earlier in the chapter. We'll give you a push start by telling you the first word was stapler but as for the rest, you're on your own. Don't move onto the next chapter until you've recalled them all.

6

Pulling the Triggers

Welcome to Chapter 6. Don't think that now you've escaped from the tests and challenges of the previous chapter that you can relax from here on to the end of the book. Because here, interspersed with some testimonies of the people who successfully use the methods that we've looked at in their day-to-day lives, we have a few more tasks for you.

First of all, here's another set of words for you to remember: fuse; adhesive tape; cup; jacket; kennel; clothes line; aerial; shoes; file; chess; fireplace; car; cinema; log; carpet. From now on until the end of the book, you'll be given periodically a set of fifteen words to learn. With each succeeding set, your ability to create vivid links between each of them should become a little easier and happen just that little bit more quickly. Now, let's see how these means of remembering and then triggering recall work in the real world.

Bill is a senior consultant with a so called 'full services marketing agency'. Full service means that rather than concentrating on one area of marketing, such as advertising, the agency has the breadth of expertise to implement for its clients a complete set of marketing techniques. In addition to advertising, this includes public relations, direct mail (junk mail to you and me), conference organization, exhibition stand design, sponsorships, video production and corporate identity (company logos and brochures). Together these different facilities are called the marketing mix.

Nowadays, in a world of ever-increasing competition, most companies, large and small, are investing an increasing percentage of their turnovers into their marketing strategies simply to keep up with the pack. There is, therefore, an increasing reliance upon marketing agencies: the public needs to be told the value of a company's product, and why it is better than an intrinsically identical product made by a competitor. With so many companies clamouring for marketing services you would think this was a mandate for marketing agencies such as Bill's to print money. However, this is far from the truth. In an overpopulated marketplace, agencies have to battle for survival, epecially as more and more advertising agencies are starting to offer a 'full service'. Consultants such as Bill, therefore, have to be very much on the ball.

'The typical way in which a client chooses an agency to work for it is with a three or four-way pitch,' explains Bill. 'This is where each agency is given a couple of hours to present a programme of activities that it feels will best market the client and the client's products to its target audience – in other words, the punters. This presentation is given to the client's marketing executives, and possibly the company's managing director.' As competition between agencies increases, so do the sums of money spent on making the presentation. Slick audio-visual displays, extensive market research and mock-ups of designs are all used.

'We were getting some business with these techniques,' continues Bill, 'but not enough to justify the expense. I felt that the more agencies spend on the slick presentations, the harder it becomes for clients to really distinguish between them, and it becomes pot luck as to which agency is chosen. So I decided that it was time for a return to basics. In the final analysis, what we have is a document detailing item by item the sort of marketing strategy we'd execute if appointed – where to advertise, where to run giveaway promotions, which event to sponsor, and so on. However, to be frank, the prospectus of one agency is not going to differ greatly from that of another's. It comes down to personalities. I have a good bunch of people working for me yet all the jazzy audiovisuals were obscuring this fact.

'At the next presentation, I looked at my colleagues as they went over what we would do for the client, speaking against a background of colourful slides, and it looked to me as if they were intimidated by it all. Their noses were in the documents and they lacked assertiveness. It was almost as if they were afraid of diverting attention away from the slides.' Bill decided there and then to strip away all the unnecessary components of the operation leaving 'just me, my colleague and the document.'

Bill felt the need to impress the prospective client with the personalities, to arrest the attention, to excite and to compel. This meant leaving the document in the briefcase until it was handed to the client at the end of the meeting, and speaking directly to the audience without notes. 'I didn't want to learn the thing by rote – it would have taken too long, it would have sounded stilted since none of is an actor and it would have looked and sounded bad if we forgot something.'

Instead, he used the link method to create a chain of visual associations from key points within the documents that would lead him through. 'We broke the document file into sections, which each of us would have to present. Once we'd worked out the key points of the whole document together, it was up to each of us to decide what sort of imagery we'd use for our own slots. One of my sections talked about the use of PRESS RELEASES (authors' emphasis). I had to say that they were relied upon TOO HEAVILY, that EDITORS quickly recognize releases with LITTLE NEWS VALUE and BIN them without reading them. Releases should only be despatched when ANNOUNCING SOMETHING NEWSWORTHY and then only at SELECTED journals.' Linking the key words, first and second, second and third and so on, Bill came up with these links:

a huge ream of PRESS RELEASES weighing down a kitchen scales (HEAVILY); a fat EDITOR complete with green sun shade; the editor holding a magnifying glass to a tiny press release (LITTLE NEWS VALUE); a gasometer-sized BIN full of crumpled press releases; the bin inverted into the shape of a megaphone with press releases shooting out (ANNOUNCING SOMETHING NEWSWORTHY); the press releases all landing on one magazine (SELECTED) amid a carpet of hundreds of them.

'That was only a tiny part of the document and at first it was hard to get the knack of laboriously going through it looking for links in everything. I really thought we were onto a loser. But as we got into the discipline, we all found ourselves conjuring up these associations faster and faster to the extent that we were creating links as we read through something for the first time without even having to go back and note the key words. And in the next presentation it worked like a dream. We didn't have to think what we were going to say, the visual links just rolled out so that we were able to concentrate on establishing a rapport with the prospective clients. And we got the business!'

Now that you've seen how the link method can be used in practice – and how it is certainly more than just a trick for learning words – here's a little exercise for you to try yourself. Read the following passage, pick out what you think are the key words and then use them to form a series of vivid visual associations. Try not to read it more than twice:

Brian met Ted Waterman who had just arrived at Birmingham New Street station from Aberdeen. Ted picked up his luggage and put it into the boot of Brian's blue Astra. Turning left out of the station they drive towards Moseley. 'I'm en route to Bath so I'll only stay the night,' said Ted as the car drove up Eucalyptus Avenue. 'I'll be staying there with Professor Braintree and helping him research his book on Roman washing habits. After that, it's down to Brighton.' The car turned right onto Ullswater Crescent and ran parallel to the canal before forking left over the bridge. Two anglers stood on the bridge, one wearing a blue quilted jacket. Immediately after the Red Lion pub on their right, they turned left down Elmwood Road, came to a roundabout, took the first left turning and drove down Brian's road, Grange Road. 'It's really good of you to put me up at short notice, Mr Vaughn,' said Ted.

Again, if we were to question you immediately after having read this little passage, you'd probably remember most of the information. The acid test, then, is to remember it when we ask you some questions about it some time from now. Right now, though, try to recall the fifteen words we gave you at the start of the chapter. The first word was fuse.

Let's look at another application for the link method. Dudley works for an organization that carries out seminars on working practices – such as effective use of time – for junior to middle level managers. Like Bill, he, too, uses the link method for his presentations from time to time if need be. On the whole, though, he is sufficiently familiar with his subject matter to be able to talk about it fluently and confidently without recourse to mental triggers.

'Where the method is constantly useful, though, is in remembering names and faces,' says Dudley. 'You have to understand that the courses I run are quite intensive. One or two-day affairs. That gives me very little time to establish a rapport with everyone. Also, some people are there under sufferance and they need to be convinced that they're going to come away with something useful. It's up to me to get their confidence and to demonstrate mine. This means, first and foremost, learning their names.'

Some tutors have attendees write their names on an upright card and ask them to stand it in front of them at their tables. Dudley prefers a subtler, and therefore more effective, approach. 'At the start of the first day, I have each attendee stand up in turn and introduce him or herself. By the time they've sat down and the next person has risen, I've been able to create a vivid mental association between their name and a distinctive feature of their physical appearance. Then when the last introduction has been made, I like to turn back to one of the more disgruntled-looking members of the seminar and say 'now such-and-such, what do you think of . . . .' Being recognized and remembered like this makes them feel a much more involved participant and I find that the barriers soon break down.

This method is precisely the same one used by Kathy, a teacher in a large West Midlands comprehensive. 'Each year I have a new class of first years to teach and each year it's the same – they're clearly intimidated by the size of the school after their junior schools, they feel a little lost, frightened and friendless.' Like Dudley, Kathy has each pupil stand up and introduce him or herself. In this way she can assimilate all their names in the space of half a lesson. 'Calling them by their first name in a friendly way is reassuring for them and I find I get a good, responsive attitude in the classroom very quickly.' Another factor at work here is that almost half of Kathy's pupils are of Asian origin – with names whose sounds are unfamiliar to her. The fact that the link method rapidly creates vivid images from these sounds is an enormous advantage.

Speaking of names, do you remember the names of the ten people we met in Chapter 5? Good, because here are their faces for you to put their names to.

The link method also has an important role to play in the groves of academe. Fran is a journalist currently working in her spare time on a degree in art history with the Open University:

'I've always loved going to galleries. I get very moved by paintings, in fact, so I thought how wonderful it would be to gain as thorough an appreciation and understanding of the medium as I could. What I didn't expect was the mass of historical details I have to learn for the course. There are hundreds of foreign – particularly Italian – quintuple-barrelled names: of patrons, teachers, pupils, obscure painters, periods, villages, pigments, schools. Learning these was a laborious bore. It wasn't fun, and since I was taking the course for my own pleasure, I was going to give up.

A workmate heard me moaning about the course in the office and mentioned the link method to me. Over lunch she told me how it works – with its silly pictures and everything – so I thought I might give it a go. The first thing I tried it on was the name of the man who commissioned Botticelli to paint his Birth of Venus, Lorenzo di Pierfrancesco de Medici. Picturing the painting, I imagined the role of Venus, standing on the shell taken by Lauren Bacall (hence Lorenzo) with San Francisco's fisherman's wharf standing in the background (pier-francesco). Obviously, it wasn't exactly right but it was such a stupid picture, I couldn't get it out of my mind and I don't think I ever will.

Since then I've used this method whenever I have new names to remember – which is very often – and it works like magic. What's more, the process of actually dreaming up these stupid pictures is a lot of fun in itself.'

Finally, before we move on to other topics, here are a few questions for you to answer:

- Can you give me directions from the station to Brian Vaughn's house?
- From the start, what is Ted Waterman's itinerary?
- What is the name of the professor he will be staying with?
- What word came: after kennel? before yo-yo? before log? after fuse? before kennel? after razor?

As stated at the start of Chapter 5, these methods can be used by people whose memories are perfectly healthy and are victims merely of lack of focus leading to poor recall. Luckily, most people's memory problems extend no further than this. Some, however, are victims of much deeper and far-reaching causes of memory loss and it is these – together with means of alleviating the problem – that we'll look at in the next chapter.

7

Supplementing your Memory

The way our health is affected by our environment is justifiably causing increasing public anxiety. Every day new and disturbing statistics are added to the mountain of evidence which shows that the declining quality of commodities we have taken for granted – beef, eggs, chicken, apples, water and even air – may be contributing to an assortment of degenerative diseases from cancer to Alzheimer's disease. The result is a succession of government ministers and health experts appearing on television and radio in an attempt to soothe concern. Their bland assurances usually take two forms: first there is the smug 'you-really-shouldn't-bother-yourselves-with-something-you-don't-understand' mode; second the 'of-course-this-country-has-the-best-health-standards-in-the-world' gambit.

City dwellers often do not recognize the sulphurous shrouds of smog that hang over most cities during the summer for what they are – instead they are looked upon as heat hazes; and while the hint of chlorine in our water supplies assures us that the water is free of bacteria, few of us realize that it remains monstrously high in inorganic nitrates, phosphates and other impurities; simultaneously, the nutritional value of our food – the vegetables covered in pesticides and bloated with fertilizers – decreases in inverse proportion to its cost-effectiveness to the farmer and cosmetic attractiveness on supermarket shelves.

Amidst this really rather parlous state of affairs, there is, thankfully, an increasing realization that each of us can do something to protect ourselves from these problems. The solution lies, at least partially, with nutritional supplementation. This means taking vitamins, minerals, amino acids and fatty acids in pill, powder or capsule form to make up for what we lose from our food and to combat the harmful effects of toxins in our environment. Of course, there are opposing arguments. Foremost among these is that a well-balanced diet provides us with the full cross-section of necessary nutrients. Therefore, what possible benefit can there be from taking supplements?

A good way of countering such blinkered certainty is to cite a concept that is currently forcing scientists to reassess the way they view the world. It is called simply 'chaos' and it states that no matter how much we may learn about a subject – whether it is weather forecasting or deciding upon our nutritional needs – no matter how deeply we think we understand it, how effectively we can even control it, we will never be able to master that subject completely. The most graphic example of this theory can be found in the science of meteorology. Today, weather-forecasters possess an impressive arsenal of the most sensitive measuring instruments. Their forecasts, it stands to reason, should therefore be all the more accurate and long-ranging. Yet, the most impressive achievement of this technology has been to more accurately define the forecasters' limitations. In other words, they are now able to predict with certainty that predicting the weather beyond four or five days into the future is a futile exercise.

The reason for this is simple, obvious and completely insurmountable. Even with radar satellites and Earth stations monitoring the minute changes of temperature, wind speed and direction across the surface of the globe, there are innumerable factors beyond the range of these instruments which will affect the weather every bit as much. Individually these facts are unimportant but together they make a mockery of a precise forecast. Thus the immeasurably small amount of turbulence caused by a butterfly fluttering its wings in Rome will eventually change the complexion of the weather in London or New York or Tokyo. For want of a nail the kingdom was lost; for want of a butterfly the forecast was lost.

Look at our nutrient needs. As we've seen, the shortage of only one essential nutrient will cause a metabolic chain reaction in our bodies similar to the effect a butterfly has on the weather. How can medical authorities claim – in the face of polluted water and air, food with its nutrients depleted – that nutritional supplementation is superfluous? In fact, it should form a central pillar of everyone's health plans.

This chapter assumes unashamedly, then, that for healthy brain function – for clear thinking and a rapid-recalling, far-reaching memory – nutritional supplementation is of enormous importance. So let's look to see which supplements we can use to energize our brain power and from this develop a structured programme of intelligent supplementation.

Fatty acids – memory lubricants

Essential polyunsaturated fatty acids play a variety of crucial roles in ensuring a healthy memory. The most prominent of these is providing nerve cells with the neurotransmitter and neuro-muscular-transmitter known as acetylcholine. Acetylcholine is made in the body from quantities of the phosphatide called lecithin and its offshoot, choline. You may remember from Chapter 3 that a phosphatide is a trident-shaped molecule formed from a fatty acid, an essential polyunsaturated fatty acid and a phosphate. The highest natural concentration of lecithin is found in eggs – in fact, the word lecithin comes from the Greek word for egg yolk. It is also found in sunflower oil, soyabean oil, and flax.

When activated in the neurons, acetylcholine triggers primitive, instinctive responses to external stimuli. These include physical preparedness in times of danger or sexual arousal. For these functions, its effects are similar to that best known of all brain chemicals, the excitory, fight-or-flight neurotransmitter, adrenalin.

However, acetylcholine is also an important component in the formation of conscious, short and long term memories. Without it, learning becomes impossible. In their book, Life Extension, Durk Pearson and Sandy Shaw report how a shortage of acetylcholine in the body contributes to forgetfulness, absent-mindedness and disorientation. Deficiency also reduces mental concentration, allowing the subject to become easily distracted by superfluous stimuli. As we saw in Chapter 2, one of the classic methods used by researchers to prevent volunteers from remembering new information is to interrupt the volunteer at the learning stage, by having them recite sequences of meaningless numbers, unrelated to the task they have been given to learn. This has the effect of breaking up an embryonic engram before it has the chance of consolidating the links between its components neurons. Exactly the same thing appears to happen with a deficiency of acetylcholine. New memories will be formed only with great difficulty and no matter how the victim concentrates on the subject at hand, he or she will experience a frustrating and sustained sense of distraction.

Acetylcholine also stimulates the secretion of a hormone from the brain's pituitary gland called vasopressin. Synthetic vasopressin is regularly administered in the United States, both nasally and orally, to patients suffering from poor memory and amnesia. Results show that it can significantly improve memory and learning ability.

The biochemical detergent

As well as acting as the parent molecule of acetylcholine, lecithin is also important for what is called its 'lipotrophic factor'. This is an ability to separate fatty substances into thin layers rather than having them gather in thick clumps. It is vitally important for the health of every cell membrane – but especially the neuron – that lecithin does this. This is because every membrane is composed primarily of fatty substances (phosphatides and triglycerides) surrounded both inside and out by water with numerous nutrients and small proteinaceous substances in suspension. With so much water about, the natural tendency of the fat in the membrane is to agglomerate in clumps – rather like oil slicks at sea. If this was allowed to happen, the membrane would lose its necessary flexibility, nutrients would be unable to pass into the cell and nerve transmissions from one cell's axon to the next cell's dendrite would go astray. The results could range from forgetfulness, disorientation and outright amnesia to hallucinations and schizophrenia.

In preventing this, the lipotrophic factor of lecithin and choline force the fat to spread out into two flexible and lubricated layers. Nerve transmissions can then pass satisfactorily between cells while each is well supplied with the nutrients it needs for growth and repair.

Cholesterol alert

The sort of problem that may arise in the cell membrane from a lack of lecithin – that is, a hardening of the cell walls due to the tendency of the fat to agglomerate in water – also occurs when too much cholesterol is allowed to enter the membrane. Originally, cholesterol plays a regulating function opposite to that of lecithin – preventing the cell from becoming too fluid, and injecting structural support into the cell wall rather like a metabolic cement. All too often, though, too much cholesterol finds its way into the membranes.

This will happen when, for instance, we get drunk: the alcohol will dilute the cell membrane causing it to become too fluid. To compensate, extra cholesterol is drawn in to provide rigidity. If you drink regularly then, even after stopping the alcohol intake, so much cholesterol will be left in the cell walls that the extra rigidity will cause symptoms similar to those of lecithin and choline deficiency. It will force you to drink alcohol simply to achieve the normal level of cell fluidity. This is why alcoholics regularly suffer from absentmindedness, amnesia, hallucinations, sensory disorientation and schizophrenia. Most people have experienced at least one night of heavy drinking where they are simply unable to remember the next day what they did. If, as an alcoholic, you suffer regularly from this syndrome, then taking lecithin and choline supplements is one of the best ways of getting a lift onto the wagon.

Of course, the problem of excess cholesterol isn't confined only to alcoholism. Many people's bodies are overburdened with cholesterol – both as a result of a poor diet and as a response to occupational stress. In time, it can lead to the formation of fatty plaques along the walls of the arteries. The resulting constriction of the blood supply could lead to atherosclerosis and arteriosclerosis – both of which have been implicated in loss of memory. Adequate lecithin and choline, however, will actually regulate the level of cholesterol in the blood as well as in the cell membranes, carrying it instead to the liver where it can be excreted into the gut.

The nerve insulators

Lecithin and choline also form part of what is known as the

myelin sheath. This is an insulating layer around each nerve cell that works in the same way as the rubber tubing that surrounds each of the earth, neutral and live wires of ordinary electrical cables. These cables would immediately short-circuit if they were allowed to contact each other without the protection of the insulators and the same holds true of our nerve cells. A rupture of the myelin sheath caused by a lecithin and choline deficiency will result in nerve messages being poorly transmitted, causing forgetfulness, amnesia, hallucinations and schizophrenia. It has also been implicated in motor neurone diseases such as multiple sclerosis and Parkinson's disease.

Why use supplements?

As we've seen, lecithin and choline are prominent components of many widely available foods. This begs the question, if it can be found in so many food sources, then why do we need to take it as a supplement? Let's find out.

Thanks to the essential polyunsaturate components of its trident-shaped configuration, lecithin is an extremely biochemically active substance. We saw in Chapter 1 how polyunsaturates are the body's tuning forks, reacting to the stimuli of touch, light and even sound by converting them to electrical impulses. Since they must respond to the lightest of touches, the dimmest of lights, the faintest of sounds, they are sensitive almost to the point of instability; any stimulus causes a reaction. Therefore, when exposed to heat, light or oxygen, they will degrade rapidly. Lecithin-rich food sources, therefore, have a very short shelf life.

This makes them unpopular with food manufacturers and supermarket stock-controllers. Their priorities, after all, are arranging convenient production and stock cycles rather than providing fresh, nutritious food. However, because of its lipotrophic factor, lecithin is an excellent emulsifier – it makes blending fat-based ingredients with water to create goods such as margarine much easier. This emulsifying effect means that manufacturers are unwilling to eradicate lecithin totally. So instead they use synthetically developed strains of lecithin containing fewer, shorter and less active varieties of polyunsaturates. This allows its emulsifying properties to be exploited without it causing the food to go rancid so quickly.

If you look at the ingredients list on many food products such as margarines, chocolates, cakes, and desserts, you'll see lecithin included. Don't be fooled into thinking that this is the nutritious, active variety; it is included solely to make the fat-based ingredients blend with the water-based counterparts.

Things are just as bad when it comes to the lecithin content of oils. Most commercially produced oils are pressed from seeds such as safflower, sunflower or grape, from beans such as soy and the flesh of certain vegetables such as olives. The huge industrial screw presses used for this task create tremendous friction, leading in turn to high temperatures. The heat then speeds up the degradation process of the essential polyunsaturated fatty acids within the oil, leading to rancidity. To overcome this problem, the oils are deodorized and sterilized. The finished product is an inert parody of a naturally nutritious oil. However, the manufacturer may still claim – and, by the strict letter of the law, be perfectly justified in doing so – that the product has been cold-pressed and is high in polyunsaturates. In fact, thanks to the processing, these polyunsaturates have mutated from their active cis (kinked) variety, to an active trans (or flat) variety which prevents them from participating in the creation of acetylcholine or any other of lecithin's important functions.

The best alternative, then, is to take lecithin and/or choline in supplement form.

Where from?

Most health food stockists or suppliers carry lecithin granules extracted from natural soya. These can be sprinkled on salads or stirred into yogurts, juices or soups. They should never be cooked with, though, as this will cause the fatty acids to degrade too rapidly. Light also causes degradation, so ensure that your container is opaque and kept in a dark place.

The amount you choose will vary depending on your perceived needs. If you feel that you need only a mental pick-me-up then try about 10 grams a day. The American nutritional expert, Richard Passwater, reports that volunteers who were fed up to 70 grams of lecithin a day were able to learn longer lists of words and numbers and recall them with a much greater degree of accuracy than before when called upon to do so.

Some people prefer to take choline rather than lecithin since – in terms of the body's metabolic pathways – it is one stage closer to acetylcholine. An average dose will vary between one and three grams a day. Another good supplement is phosphatidyl choline which is, in effect, a lecithin supplement that contains three times the ordinary amount of choline.

To sum up, lecithin and choline are needed for:
1 the formation of the memory and learning neurotransmitter, acetylcholine
2 lubricating and maintaining flexibility in the neuron membranes – guaranteeing that nerve impulses are transmitted accurately from cell to cell and that each nerve is adequately fed
3 regulating the body's cholesterol levels, both in the nerve membrane and in the blood vessels that feed the brain, thus preventing plaque build-up that may in time threaten the memory
4 insulating individual neurons to prevent nerve messages from becoming crossed.

The value of these chemicals as an aid to improving memory is graphically illustrated by the experience of a young woman called Julie. A keen outward bound instructor, Julie was recently involved in a near tragedy when she fell nearly a hundred feet down a sheer rock face on a climb she was leading. She was saved from certain death by the belay rope but even so suffered severe concussion and was kept in a darkened hospital room for a month. Several months after leaving hospital she became conscious of startling lapses of memory. Yawning gaps opened up in her recall of events since her accident; she couldn't, for example, remember at which hospital she had been treated. She would set out from home to see a friend only to find that she couldn't remember where she was going. Sometimes she forgot what she was saying in mid-sentence. Worse still, at work her colleagues began to notice a slackness in her preparation of equipment for dangerous and safety-critical activities, coupled with a vague, imprecise attitude when instructing her parties.

'When I look back on it now, I seem to see it all as if I were living in a fog that slightly obscured reality,' she recalls. 'I was walking around in that rather delicious moment just before you drop off into a very deep sleep – very drowsy, very heavy – yet this was during the daytime when I was meant to be instructing people whose lives depended on my mental clarity.' Recognizing the potential danger, her manager made her take a further month's sick leave, during which time she came for nutritional counselling. She was put on a course of 50 grams of lecithin daily, together with vitamins B_3, B_6 and folic acid, each of which are essential for brain function. 'Within days that fog seemed to lift. I was incisive, well organized and in total control. The change was amazing.' Now that we've seen what fats can do, let's look at the other major group of organic components – amino acids.

Amino acids – a mental fuel injection

While amino acids are usually described as the building blocks of protein, the jobs they carry out in the body are far more complex and varied than simply providing the metabolic 'brickwork' of tissue. They are also used to render harmful toxins inert so that they can safely be excreted from the body; they form enzymes – the special carrier molecules which bring different substances together in chemical reactions to form new structures; and they make up the bulk of the brain's neurotransmitters. In fact, amino acids are used so widely in the brain – both as components of protein and in their own right – that deficiencies are widely thought to contribute to memory loss.

Amino acid supplementation has grown in popularity over the last few years and today most nutritionalists enthusiastically recommend their use. The advantage of taking amino acids over eating ordinary foods high in protein is that, while protein must be laboriously digested before being absorbed, amino acids pass rapidly through the gut lining and circulate to wherever they are needed. If, as Chris Reading suggests (see page 45), Alzheimer's disease is related to poor digestion and absorption of vital nutrients, then amino acids can obviously make an important contribution to rectifying possible nutrient shortfalls.

The supplements are widely available from health food shops and mail order suppliers. When choosing, however, make sure that the product you buy is called a 'free form amino acid' rather than a protein powder. While the powders are protein-enriched they will need digesting before they are absorbed, somewhat defeating the object of the exercise. As far as dosage is concerned, follow the instructions on the canister, and if there is no obvious change in your well-being, slowly increase the amount. Since amino acids are simply the purest forms of food, rather than a medicine, you can ingest quite high amounts without any ill-effects. However, if you are pregnant or lactating, or if you use MAO inhibitors as an antidepressant, we recommend that you seek the approval of a health professional before using any of these supplements. Now, let's see how amino acid supplementation can improve your memory.

Waste disposal aminos

The first amino acid we'll look at is called glutamine. Its most important effect on brain function is that it prevents the build-up of a potentially lethal poison – ammonia. Wait a minute, just what is ammonia doing in the brain in the first place? As the centre for 25 per cent of the body's entire metabolic activity, the brain produces large amounts of waste by-products. After all, memory formation and the transmission of nerve impulses from one cell to the next is a never ending process of creating new proteins from their constituent amino acids. This protein is used up at a phenomenal pace. Rather than simply excrete the exhausted protein, it is instead split up back into its constituent aminos and these in turn are split open to release energy for powering the metabolic pathways. However, the one problem with this otherwise marvellously economic use of the body's resources is that it produces large amounts of leftover ammonia.

Normally this ammonia is removed safely from the brain thanks to the action of an amino acid called glutamic acid which dumps it in the urine. However, due to nutritional shortfall – and this is especially common in times of sustained physical or mental stress – there is not enough glutamic acid to convert the ammonia. Instead it is allowed to build up in the brain and, if unchecked, can cause irritability, tremors, vomiting, hallucinations, amnesia and eventually death. Forgetfulness is a common response to stress and this increase in the brain's ammonia levels is one of the key reasons. It also creates a spiral of deficiency since, in a stressed state, any forgetfulness is only likely to make you feel even more stressed.

This is where glutamine supplementation comes in. Once in the brain, it is converted to glutamic acid where it reinvigorates the ammonia-detoxifying process. Tests show that it increases alertness, mental clarity and the ability to store and recall greater amounts of information.

The nutrition expert, Richard Passwater, has found that glutamine also acts in the brain in a similar way to glucose – providing fuel energy for increased metabolic activity. Glutamine, therefore, can be seen as the memory's turbo-charger. Many students, particularly in the USA, now use glutamine when revising for exams. Unlike caffeine, glutamine unleashes the natural energies within the brain. Finally, glutamine also helps to form folic acid – a B vitamin that is itself used widely in the brain for the maintenance of the memory functions.

Aminos and Alzheimer's

Amino acids are also becoming recognized as a valuable weapon in the war against Alzheimer's disease. The first inkling of the therapeutic effects of amino acids came in the late 1960s and early 1970s at the Brain Bio Institute in Princeton – a nutritional research body headed by one of the field's towering figures, Carl Pfeiffer. While researching into the causes of Alzheimer's disease, he examined brain tissue from a large number of victims' brains in order to measure the degrees of arteriosclerosis and atherosclerosis – the artery-clogging and hardening disease that were felt to be major contributory factors. To his surprise, only a third of the Alzheimer patients he examined showed any symptoms of either arteriosclerosis or atherosclerosis.

Clearly there were other causes. Pfeiffer quickly discovered instead that every patient had exceedingly low levels of an amino acid derivative called spermine. Spermine is used in the brain as a component of an enzyme called RNA polymerase. It is this enzyme which brings together a number of separate chemicals to fashion RNA. As we've already seen, RNA is vital for the formation of memory. Any shortage causes memory loss. To his delight, he found that when supplemented with the amino acid precursors to spermine, the patients showed a marked improvement in their ability to memorize and recall information.

The precursors of spermine are an essential amino acid (that is, one that cannot be made in the body from sufficient quantities of other aminos) called arginine, together with another called methionine which helps transform arginine in the metabolic pathways. Vitamin B_6 was also important. One word of warning: arginine has been found to stimulate cold sores – assuming that you already have the virus. Therefore, if you suffer from this complaint, it's best to take an amino acid called ornithine. Ornithine is one step along from arginine in the metabolic pathway that creates spermine.

Galvanized aminos

Two more important amino acids are phenylalanine (another essential) and its derivative, tyrosine. These are the precursors of a set of neurotransmitters called the catecholamines, the best known of which is the hormone adrenalin. Adrenalin, secreted from the adrenal gland sitting atop the liver, is an excitory neurotransmitter. It provides physical arousal and alertness, galvanizing often torpid individuals into a far more positive frame of mind. For many people, an inability to store or recall memories is caused by depression. We saw in Chapter 5 how much easier it becomes to remember information if we give it special importance or significance. In a depressed state, however, it is very difficult to see anything as important or meaningful. Phenylalanine and tyrosine help to lift individuals out of this state of mind, giving a more positive, pronounced and decisive outlook on life.

Complete blend – total memory

Since the process of memory formation and learning is such a large consumer of protein – with its unceasing secretion of neurotransmitters and constant strengthening of the physical bonds between the participating neurons in an engram – many nutritionists now recommend a supplement of all 22 amino acids blended together in one preparation. This, in effect, provides a complete nutritional base for whatever proteins your brain needs to manufacture. The complete blend is used to complement, rather than replace, the individual amino acids we've looked at.

To sum up, amino acids are important to the memory because:

1 glutamine removes the toxin ammonia – waste product of protein metabolism – from the sensitive brain tissue
2 glutamine is a brain fuel
3 glutamine helps to synthesize folic acid
4 arginine (or ornithine) and methionine help to improve memory by producing spermine, which in turn helps to create RNA
5 phenylalanine and tyrosine provide greater alertness and mental vitality
6 the complete blend helps to support protein formation throughout the brain.

How effective these supplements are is shown by the experiences of a bank manager called Liz who came for nutritional counselling complaining of a progressive loss of memory. 'The most important ability in my line of work is to be able to remember figures and faces,' she says. 'And I couldn't remember either. Things had been getting worse for months but in the nature of things, if it doesn't happen suddenly you don't notice it because it's too gradual. Then, one day I was having a meeting with one of my small-business managers. We were reviewing the quarterly forecasts when, half way through the meeting, I realized I could hardly remember anything I'd read. Worse, for a moment I couldn't even place the face of the man next to me – yet we'd worked together for 18 months. I though, "This is it girl, you've got Alzheimer's disease!"'

Luckily for her, it was nowhere near as serious. Under further counselling, Liz admitted that she recently had been under terrific stresses in her home life. She and her husband had lately separated. Almost at the same time, her father, with whom she was very close, had suffered a stroke, rendering him unable to communicate with anyone. 'Everything was falling down around my ears,' she recalled. Not surprisingly, Liz hadn't been greatly concerned about her diet during this period and with the stresses both at home and at work, nutritional deficiency had become inevitable. To compensate, Liz was given a course of glutamine and phenylalanine, together with the complete blend. After only a matter of days, she reported a rapid improvement. 'Things are so much more vivid now,' she says. ' I don't seem to have to make any more effort now than I did when I couldn't remember a thing, it's just that everything seems to lodge in my mind's eye like a shining jewel. It's wonderful.'

Each of the nutritional supplements mentioned in this chapter is best taken with complementary co-factors. These are substances that assist your body in utilizing the nutrients to their fullest potential. These co-factors are vitamins and minerals and in Chapter 8 we'll see which ones are best for your memory.

8

Supplemental Support

The substances that we'll look at in this chapter should, as we suggested, be used to complement the fat and protein-based supplements that we looked at in the last chapter. However, many people also take them as supplements in their own right, claiming considerable therapeutic benefit in doing so. There is no hard and fast rule as to how much of a particular vitamin or mineral you should take, but it is generally advisable to follow the instructions on the canister and only raise your intake on the advice of a health professional.

Perhaps the most important of the complementary co-factors are the B vitamins, all of which play important roles in assisting brain and nerve metabolism. While they are found in abundance in most foods, vitamin B deficiency is thought to be quite common. Refining and cooking destroys much of the food's content of both the separate B vitamins and B complex (the naturally-occurring blend of all the B vitamins, found especially in yeast and liver). The more starchy food which is eaten, the greater the demands will be on the body's available B stock. This is because one of their important roles is to convert carbohydrate into usable forms of energy. The more white bread and cake you eat, therefore, the greater the depletion of B vitamins will become – especially if the rest of your food is overcooked. Such warnings were until recently dismissed as scare stories but the recurrence today of many B deficiency-related diseases such as rickets and beriberi in deprived areas of industrial countries such as Britain has shown just how easily such deficiencies can arise.

Apart from releasing valuable sources of energy, B vitamins perform other important tasks such as overhauling our vital organs – especially the liver – and maintaining the lubricity of the mucous membranes. However, their most important function as far as we're concerned is the way they help to maintain the health and efficiency of the brain and central nervous system. Vitamin B deficiency, it seems, mimics, if not creates, a wide range of symptoms typical of senility. These range from mild disorientation and forgetfulness to hallucinations, paranoia and profound amnesia.

This in fact raises another issue, namely the importance of nutrition to the elderly. After our mid-twenties, our calorie needs decrease by approximately one per cent a year, with this percentage increasing exponentially among the elderly. As the need for calories declines, so does the amount of nutritious food which people eat. Paradoxically, it is the group which eats the least food – the elderly – which needs the greatest concentration of health-giving nutrients to sustain the battle against problems such as senility and forgetfulness. Furthermore, the elderly tend to prefer their food well-cooked so that it can easily be eaten. These trends lead inexorably to a loss of B vitamins. The alternative, then, is clearly to supplement potential victims – old or young – with these nutrients.

Vitamin B_1 is a prime example of the importance of B vitamins for memory. Otherwise known as thiamine, it is found in high concentrations within the nervous system. Its importance for neural health is shown by the fact that it is used with some success to treat victims of multiple sclerosis. Furthermore, tests with rats have found that it plays a vital role in improving short term memory. Victims of acute memory loss and senility, on the other hand, are regularly found to be low in thiamine.

Vitamins B_2 (riboflavin) and B_3 play similarly important roles. For example, Abram Hoffer, one of Canada's foremost experts on the effect of nutrition on health, found that senile patients in mental hospitals responded positively to enormous levels of B_3 supplementation – up to 500 times the recommended daily amounts. When the amounts administered were dropped below this level their symptoms of hallucinations, delusions, forgetfulness and disorientation gradually returned.

B_3 is a near-ubiquitous component of the body's metabolic pathways and helps the amino acid glutamine to get rid of ammonia from the brain. Unlike B_1 and B_2 it comes as a supplement in several different forms – niacin, nicotinamide and nicotinic acid – which for our purposes all have the same result. The acid form, though, will cause you to blush and tingle but this is a perfectly normal reaction and nothing to be concerned about. As for the other B vitamins, the most important for nerve function are thought to be B_6 and folic acid. Probably the simplest way of taking the B vitamins is with an all-inclusive B complex supplement together with additional supplements of those vitamins that you feel are most important.

C change

Apart from the B complex, the most important vitamin for brain health, indeed for total health, is vitamin C. Humans, primates, and most monkeys lost the ability to manufacture vitamin C in their bodies millions of years ago, which is a great shame. All other mammals, with the exceptions of a fruit eating bat and the guinea pig, can manufacture vitamin C in relatively large quantities. Perhaps the most important of its many vital roles is as a component of collagen, the latticework protein structure on which the entire human body, including bones, hangs. It is also a powerful antioxidant and free radical scavenger, protecting the super-polyunsaturated fatty acids from degradation and rancidity. Any nutritional supplementation, no matter what it is, should include vitamin C. The intake recommended by the UK Ministry of Agriculture, Fisheries and Food is pitifully low – a mere 350 milligrams. Considering that one cigarette will destroy about 25 milligrams-worth of Vitamin C, even passive smoking will obviously cause major depletion. Some nutritionists recommend amounts of ten or more grams a day, much to the scabrous mirth of health experts in conventional medicine. Still, he who laughs last, laughs longest.

Memory and the minerals

Foremost among the minerals when you are considering memory-enhancing supplements is zinc. Zinc is an important component in the growth and repair of every cell. In particular, it helps to manufacture an enzyme called DNA-dependent RNA polymerase. This is the bonding agent that clamps the blank RNA to the parent DNA prior to replication. For this reason, all protein metabolism – from the creation of enzymes and neurotransmitters to the manufacture of tissue for skin, hair and bones – needs zinc.

Zinc is a relatively fragile nutrient that is easily displaced from the body. It is antagonized by too much calcium, phosphorus and, especially, copper. The high levels of copper in cigarette smoke provide a particularly vivid picture of the effects of zinc depletion. Here, loss of zinc from lung tissue – which, after all, has the most intensive contact with copper of any of the organs – leads to inadequate healing, repair and replenishment. The effects on the gossamer, elastic folds of tissue in the lungs eventually causes hardening and is thought to be one of the main causes of emphysema. Imagine what a loss of zinc causes in the brain where RNA and protein replenishment is of paramount importance for the neural circuits, better known as engrams.

Zinc is concentrated in two places – the male prostate gland and the hypothalamus (seat of short term memory) in both men and women. Very little research has been carried out to discover the effects of zinc depletion on the hypothalamus. However, bearing in mind how close the prostate gland is to men's hearts – and other areas – a considerably greater amount of work has been conducted into the effects of depletion here. Since tests show that zinc supplementation mitigates up to two-thirds of all prostate disorders, it's likely that the mineral also has some bearing on the healthy functioning of the hypothalamus.

The levels of zinc in your body can be determined by a simple little test developed by Derek Bryce-Smith of Reading University. He has discovered that, since zinc is required in our taste buds to enhance our sense of taste, a special zinc solution swished around in the mouth will provide either a strong, medium or weak taste depending on the body's zinc levels. The less zinc in your body, the less discernible the taste. The test is available from many alternative health practitioners.

To sum up, zinc is required for the continued regeneration of protein structures throughout the body, but particularly in the brain where memories are formed. If you feel you may be suffering from zinc deficiency, then probably the best supplement to take is zinc citrate, an easily absorbed form of citric acid. The standard amount to take is 15mg a day.

Magnesium

Like zinc, magnesium is also concerned with the manufacture of proteins from DNA and RNA. And, also like zinc, it is an important co-factor in the creation of many enzymes. One particularly important chemical process in which magnesium is a co-factor is the production of the excitory neurotransmitter adrenalin from the parent molecules, phenylalanine and tyrosine. As we saw, shortages of these chemicals can lead to depression and slow-wittedness which may, in turn, cause absentmindedness and loss of memory. Alcohol, stress, diuretics and the antagonistic effects of too much calcium and phosphorus in the diet all lead to magnesium deficiency.

Magnesium also has a calming effect on the nerves, in this case working in balance with its sometime antagonist, calcium. While it is the ionic interchange between sodium and potassium that generates the electrical current for transmitting nerve messages along the neurons, calcium and magnesium control the strength of that current. In its ionic form, calcium is concentrated outside the neurons, while magnesium is found inside. Together, the two act in a similar way to the large grey transformers you see outside large buildings and guarded behind steel fences on the edge of towns.

Transformers receive electricity from the national supply and reduce its electro-motive force (EMF) – or the strength of the current – to manageable levels. After all, the force required to push electricity around the national supply network is far greater than that required to light and heat a building – or a town for that matter. If the EMF wasn't reduced by the transformer, it would burn the building down; street lamps would explode on their poles; manhole covers would blow off the pavement and television screens would disintegrate in a shower of sparks. In the same way that a transformer prevents too much electricity going where it shouldn't, calcium and magnesium control the strength of electrical transmissions within the nerves: calcium, in fact, acts as the excitor – in effect turning up the strength of the transmission – magnesium as the inhibitor turning it down. These functions are vitally important for thought and memory and if the balance between excitor and inhibitor is disrupted – either by a deficiency or excess of one or the other – then nerve signals become scrambled. This can lead to physical convulsions, poor memory, confusion, disorientation and paranoia. Today, magnesium is widely recommended both as a tranquillizer and as a means of helping to enhance memory.

Recommended daily amounts of magnesium vary from country to country but a good start is to take 250–400mg of elemental magnesium a day.

It now appears that magnesium deficiency is much more common than calcium deficiency. Many victims of neural imbalances find that simply adding magnesium supplements to their diet without any extra calcium brings about dramatic improvement. It is possible, though, to obtain a supplement which blends the two minerals in ideal proportions. This is called dolomite, a naturally-occurring mineral that contains ample amounts of both elements. Unfortunately, many nutritionists, including myself, strongly refuse to recommend this supplement, since it is often found to contain dangerously high levels of lead. Furthermore, the minerals which dolomite contains are also the inorganic forms and those who most need these minerals are usually those least able to metabolize these particular forms. On balance, it is much more advisable to take separate supplements of organic magnesium and calcium. It is also a good idea to back this up with a complementary supplement of vitamin D. This vitamin, also known as calciferol, acts as a sort of insurance policy to make sure that calcium is utilized properly. At normal levels, vitamin D acts to store whatever calcium is not required safely in the bones, rather than allowing it to circulate in the blood where it could contribute to plaque build-up. Vitamin D is sometimes called the sunshine vitamin, since it is produced in the body by the action of sunlight. There are suggestions that black people, hailing from an Afro-Caribbean background, have stronger and heavier bones than white people because of this.

Vitamin D also helps the body to store another important mineral: phosphorus. Phosphorus is important since it is needed in the formation of the fat-based nerve cell components, the phosphatides – particularly phosphatidyl choline. However, unlike some of the minerals and vitamins we've examined, there is little danger of phosphorus shortage in today's diets – especially since it is used as an acidity regulator in fizzy drinks. Certain lecithin supplements do contain phosphorus to assist with metabolism but this is all.

All these supplements, and many more, can be obtained in your local health food shop or from the following suppliers:

Cantassium
Larkhall Laboratories
225 Putney Bridge Road
London SW15 2PY
(01) 870 0971

GR Lane
Sissons Road
Gloucester

Natural Flow
Burwash Common
East Sussex
(0435) 882482

Nature's Best
PO Box 1
Tunbridge Wells
Kent TN2 3EQ
(0892) 34143

Nature's Own
Cheltenham
Glos GL50 1HX

Nutri-tec
17 Pershore Road South
Kings Norton
Birmingham
B30 3FF

Quest Vitamins
Unit 1
Premier Trading Estate
Dartmouth Middleway
Birmingham B7 4AT

Medabolics
925 Hillcrest
Paradise, California
95969
USA

Finally, here are some more memory tests for you:

Who commissioned Botticelli to paint *The Birth of Venus*? What was the object two words before cassette recorder? Which road did Brian and Ted drive down before Elmwood Road?

Give yourself no more than five minutes to memorize the following list then get a friend to test you:

Vortex; Zebra; Crank; Apple; Lattice; Crude; Wart; Lump; Fruit; Ranch; Date; Gross; Pain; Profile; Access; Yellow; Cucumber; Nose; Bowl; Spectacles.

Which name belongs to each of the following five faces?

9

Aluminium Eradication

In Chapter 4 we scrutinized the link between Alzheimer's disease and aluminium. At the end of that chapter we conceded that any evidence linking aluminium with the disease was circumstantial. Indeed, it does seem somewhat odd to suggest that the third most abundant substance on this planet behind oxygen and silicon could be harmful. Eight per cent of the world is composed of aluminium, and if it were a threat to health there would surely be a volume of incontrovertible evidence by now to prove it.

If the issue wasn't so clouded, if those researchers conducting work in the possibility of aluminium intoxication weren't portrayed as operating on the periphery of respectable work, that evidence might now exist. The truth is that since aluminium is the most widely used non-ferrous metal in the world, a great deal of time, passion and ingenuity has been invested by various interested bodies in convincing the public that aluminium is perfectly safe. The building and automotive industries, food conglomerates, kitchenware manufacturers, toiletry purveyors and water companies employ aluminium in enormous quantities. Is it any wonder that they are dedicated to using every means at their disposal to insist that it is a useful, labour saving, and harmless substance?

Putting the case most forcefully for the metal in the UK is the Aluminium Federation (ALFED), a group formed from many of the largest producers and users of aluminium. ALFED exists to promote the metal in all its forms, not merely to defend it against the health lobby, but it does produce well researched and clearly argued papers which, to the average reader, will quickly dispel any anxiety that may have arisen. Stories such as the scandalous dumping of 20 tonnes of aluminium sulphate in Cornwall are airily dismissed as if the fact that no adverse effects have yet become apparent means that they never will. Brushed aside with equal aplomb are the findings by researchers as renowned as Donald Crapper at Toronto University which, if not actually claiming to have found aluminium with its hands around the proverbial smoking gun, as least points to it as a prime suspect in the search to find the cause of Alzheimer's disease.

One of ALFED's most impressively argued pieces can be found in a paper entitled 'Aluminium and Health' (available from ALFED, Broadway House, Calthorpe Road, Fiveways, Birmingham B15 1TN. tel 021 456 1103). In a calm, cogent manner, this aims to dispel 'some of the myths and misconceptions that have recently been circulating which claim to connect aluminium and health'. In this paper, reprinted from *Aluminium News*, the author, secretary general of ALFED, David Harris, concludes that the 'evidence linking aluminium to Alzheimer's disease is conflicting and inconclusive.' The body's natural defences and filtering mechanisms are sufficient to get rid of any traces of the metal that may enter, he says, either in the faeces or urine. One issue he doesn't broach is that a surprisingly large number of people cannot properly screen themselves from contaminants in this way. As people age, their digestive system (effectively the front line of the immune system) declines in efficiency, and enzyme and acid secretion drops. In some cases the gut lining loses its impermeability. We've already looked at Chris Reading's work that suggests that Alzheimer's may be linked with a leaky bowel. If so, then the fact that it will admit aluminium could be highly relevant, turning the ALFED argument on itself.

A few months before David Harris's article appeared, a gathering of some of the best and most respected exponents of nutritional health met at a talk organized by the British Society of Nutritional Medicine. The talk was given by Neil Ward, a professor at Surrey University and a man who, more than most, has carried out sterling work to expose the menaces of heavy metal toxicity.

Addressing the audience, Ward conceded the lack of statistical evidence linking Alzheimer's to aluminium. 'Hands up,' he said, 'everyone who thinks that a link exists between aluminium and Alzheimer's.' Almost everyone in the audience put their hands up. Many of those present are at the forefront of research into means of combating the disease. Collectively they treat hundreds of patients a year. Symptoms are exhaustively matched against possible treatments. They all knew that no direct evidence could link metal to disease. Neither did they have axes to grind. Yet still these rational men and women believed that aluminium holds a key to arresting Alzheimer's disease.

What you choose to believe is up to you. You can carry on with your life in an environment packed with aluminium products and foods with a high aluminium content. Perhaps in a few years' time research may prove conclusively and irrefutably that there is no link. Alternatively, you can take certain measures to raise your body's defences against it – adopting, in effect, an aluminium elimination programme. If, in the meantime, further research surfaces to show that aluminium does indeed have a bearing on the development of Alzheimer's disease, then your stance will have been vindicated. If yours is the second choice of the two, read on.

The aluminium elimination programme follows the steps of a three-stage alert: green, amber and red. Green is the relatively simple and straightforward process of removing as many items or sources of aluminium as you can from your environment. Amber is having to undergo tests to determine the level of aluminium in your body. Red forms the measures you can adopt to lower those levels if they prove to be disturbingly high. So let's examine each measure in turn:

Green alert

There are so many aluminium-containing items which, in an ordinary modern existence we can hardly help but use, that an aluminium-free life is nearly impossible to achieve. What you can do instead is target and eradicate aluminium in your food, medicines, cooking utensils, water and toiletries.

Food

Aluminium is used as an additive in a wide variety of processed foods to speed up and simplify the manufacturing cycles. Aluminium sulphate, for example, is widely used as a raising agent in bread and cake baking. Since the labelling on the food we buy is far from comprehensive, it's often impossible to know whether the product you are buying contains aluminium or not. The safest thing to do, then, is, if in doubt, simply don't buy it. Instead, buy fresh fruits and vegetables – preferably organic. Cook with fresh foods as often as possible and buy your bread and flour in your local health food shop. All this must sound terribly glib – particularly if you have a large family which runs only by virtue of a range of quickly prepared convenience foods; or youngsters who complain when they are presented with wholemeal bread or an apple instead of a sweet or a cake; or a housekeeping budget that simply won't extend that far; or if you live on your own and simply can't be bothered to spend a lot of time cooking only for yourself. All we can say is, try your best.

Medicine

Aluminium in its hydroxide form is a major component of many antacid preparations and thousands of ulcer patients take it without a break for months on end. If you suffer from acid indigestion or peptic ulcers, then we suggest you attempt to penetrate to the root of your problems rather than temporarily hiding the symptoms with medicines – again, no easy task. However, no illness occurs in isolation. Any disorder – whether it's measles or appendicitis or, as in this case, digestive trouble, has an underlying cause. One of the best ways of tackling this is with nutritional supplementation, and to start with we recommend the complete amino acid blend that we met in Chapter 7. It's not cheap and its results won't be as immediate as the antacid but for a deep, thorough invigoration of your digestive system, regenerating powerful acids and enzymes, it's impossible to match. And, if you feel the need to continue in the short term with an antacid, ask your pharmacist to recommend a non-aluminium variety.

Cooking

Be wary, too, of aluminium cookware. The amounts of the metal that you'll remove inadvertently from the cookware when using it, and consequently ingest, will vary greatly depending on the type of food you are cooking. The greater the acid content of the food, the more aluminium will be removed: 100 grams of broccoli, for instance, has been found to remove less than one-tenth the quantity of aluminium particles removed by stewing apples – a high acid food. Again, you must measure the practicality and economics of using cheap, durable aluminium cookware against the cost of replacing it with the more expensive alternatives such as cast iron or ceramic.

Toiletries

Aluminium will also be found in many deodorants and antiperspirants. Since the skin is a semi-permeable membrane, there is a good chance that some aluminium will find its way into the blood. As the awareness of the effects of aluminium increases, many women's and men's fashion magazines are now listing the increasingly long line of aluminium-free alternatives. If in doubt, most health food stores and many speciality stores and chains usually carry a range of fragrant toiletries distilled from natural herbs and spices that provide satisfying alternatives to conventional toiletries.

Water

Perhaps the greatest single cause of concern is the level of aluminium to be found in the water supplies. As we've already seen, sterile water – that is, water free of bacteria and viruses should not be confused with pure water – that is, water free of contaminants such as nitrates, lead and aluminium. Our water today might on the whole be sterile but it is by no means pure.

As we've mentioned, acid fruits and vegetables can remove aluminium particles from the cookware surfaces and much the same principle holds true for our water supplies. We obtain our water from reservoirs which are fed in turn by rivers and streams. These are created by tributaries draining off the land following a rainfall – a land which, as we've already seen, is naturally high in aluminium. One of the main varieties of pollution is acid rain caused by plumes of sulphur dioxide and nitrous oxide billowing into the atmosphere from our fossil fuel power stations. Once airborne, these clouds react with sunlight and water vapour to create sulphuric and nitric acid respectively. Then, when this falls on the land, the acidic rain dislodges aluminium from the soil – in the same way that acidic apple removes aluminium from the saucepan – and this in time flushes into our water supplies.

To compensate, many people now use bottled water and jug filters as substitutes for drinking water obtained from the tap. However, although both alternatives are preferable to tap water, they are not ideal solutions (excuse the pun). In terms of sheer practicality it can become tiresome to fill and refill a jug every time you need fresh water (which you might forget to do anyway) or use bottled water which may cost 50p or more a litre. This is why increasingly people are installing large water filters as an integral part of their kitchen plumbing. Such filters consist primarily of a series of porous clay 'candles' through which the mains water runs. Most of the impurities are deposited on the clay leaving the water almost completely sediment-free. The prices of these filters vary but they are available from as little as £100 and are as easy to fit as the washing machine pipe.

Amber alert

Suppose you have reason to believe that you have been contaminated with excessive aluminium levels. Then again, suppose you simply want to make sure that you haven't been. How do you go about it? Fortunately, there are now several accurate but simple and non-invasive tests that you can have carried out. Let's look at them.

Hair analysis

'Hair' says Richard Passwater in his excellent book, *Trace Elements and Hair Analysis,* 'is permanently recording the past events of your elemental status.' Every strand of hair on your skin is literally a metabolic readout of how well or unwell you are. Scalp hair grows at the rate of approximately six inches a year. Like every regenerating, organic structure, if it is to grow, minute proportions of all the substances in your body – proteins, vitamins, fats and minerals – are required to manufacture the proteinaceous strands of keratin. As more of these components are added to the hair at its root, so the tip grows. Obviously, however much of a particular substance finds its way into the hair depends on its levels in the body. Therefore, the more aluminium there is to be deposited from the blood, the higher its levels will appear in the hair.

Hair analysis also presents a continuous, developing picture of your state of health, revealing trends and highlighting particular circumstances. If, for example, your hair shows a sudden increase in aluminium over the past three months, then you can trace your activities over that period to detect what the source of the contamination might be.

In many circumstances, hair analysis presents an ambiguous picture of your mineral status since the fragile antagonistic relationship between the minerals can distort the findings (does elevated calcium, for example, indicate that you have too much calcium in the body or not enough magnesium or vitamin D to help metabolize it?). However, since the very presence of certain minerals indicates toxicity regardless of their levels, hair analysis is probably the best test available for determining the presence of aluminium.

Dr Jeffrey Bland, professor of nutritional biochemistry at the University of Tacoma in Washington, suggests that aluminium readings in the hair above 60ppm (parts per million) indicate a burden on the body. He has described a case history of a woman taking a regular antacid treatment high in aluminium whose hair levels under analysis revealed similarly high levels of aluminium in her body – well in excess of 60ppm. When she stopped taking the antacids, her hair readings gradually returned to a normal level of something under 10ppm. No suggestion was made in this case that the aluminium interfered with her memory or general brain function. It does, however, lead us to a rather sinister conclusion and one that ALFED would hotly deny. Conventional wisdom has it that nearly all of the aluminium we ingest is efficiently excreted. Yet Bland clearly showed that aluminium in the woman's antacid treatment remained in her body and actually accumulated. Could this mean that we are more vulnerable to aluminium than is widely admitted?

Since for the sake of this chapter we're concerned with one substance only – aluminium – rather than adjudging how the metabolic profile as a whole is performing, hair analysis forms your best line of enquiry. The notice board of your local health food shop should be able to provide you with the address of a practitioner. When supplying hair for testing, it's best to cut a lock from lower down the back of the head. This hair grows more quickly than anywhere else on the body and it is also easiest to disguise when you cut a lock from close to the scalp. One precaution is not to supply hair that has been bleached or that you have recently washed with a high-selenium shampoo such as Selsun. Hair analysis does provide problems for men who are completely bald. Luckily there are other tests, although they only provide an insight into the body's current status – unlike the cumulative picture revealed by hair. Let's see what they are:

Blood testing

This is usually initiated by your doctor who, having obtained a blood sample with the use of a syringe, will send it away for laboratory analysis. This is not the best means of testing for aluminium since the body tends to deposit toxic contaminants in the bones, hair and nails rather than having them interfere with the precious enzyme structures suspended in the blood. An indication of low aluminium in the blood, therefore, won't necessarily mean that your body is low in aluminium as a whole.

Urine testing

The same holds true for this test. Say, for example, the urine test shows that the woman taking her antacids was excreting considerable amounts of aluminium. The natural conclusion to draw would be that her kidneys were admirably performing their designated roles and that the ingested metal was being disposed of quickly and efficiently. Yet all it takes is a fraction of that aluminium to remain in the body for it to reach high levels over a relatively short period of time. Such an accumulation can only be revealed by hair analysis.

Saliva testing

This is currently being developed and tested by a radical group of nutritionists. Here, a gobbet of saliva is wiped onto a microscope slide and fixed with a special solution, then sent for laboratory analysis. The results are thought to be much more accurate than blood or urine testing, although like those two, it can only present the body's current metabolic status.

Sweat test

Sweat is taken from a type of sticking plaster/bandaid taped to a person's back for one hour. The moisture that is gathered is analysed for a variety of minerals. Aluminium is one of the many tested.

Red alert

The result of your hair analysis arrives. You are found to have abnormally high levels of aluminium. What do you do? First, you systematically make a list of all the possible sources of high aluminium intake and remove them. Pots and pans, deodorants, products with white flour, antacids. If possible fit a water filter. Is this locking the stable door after the horse has bolted? Absolutely not. Methods actually exist for physically, though non-intrusively, removing the aluminium from your body.

Robert Erdmann writes:

At this point I want to bring in a personal experience to explain what you can do to get rid of excessive aluminium. In 1985, I became conscious of suffering from frequent occurrences of absentmindedness. I was clearly not as decisive as normal and was experiencing great difficulty concentrating and with name recall. One or two of my friends that I mentioned this to told me to relax, take it easy, that it was just a sign that I was starting to slow down as a result of ageing. As I was working long hours, this advice seemed to make sense, yet accepting their assertions ran counter to my beliefs and nutritional practice. I had long felt that as long as my metabolism was supported by optimum levels of nutrition, both from my diet and the dietary supplements I take daily, my body might get older but I would still be able to resist the ravages of ageing. I was certainly not prepared to slip gracefully into dotage. I had to do something.

Fortunately, I routinely have hair analysis and other metabolic tests. It had been 8 months since my last one. Suddenly, my aluminium levels in hair, sweat and blood were so elevated that the doctor doing the blood work-up made the written query on the report, 'Does this patient show any signs of mental problems?'

Having years ago removed all common sources of aluminium from my intake, I believed my intake was very low. Yet suddenly with no apparent explanation, I had extreme elevations in body fluids and tissue. Putting two and two together, I realized the source of aluminium must have been a temporary cap that my dentist had fitted over a cracked tooth. The cap had been replaced, but now I had to solve the problem of reversing the high concentrations of aluminium. This was accomplished by the use of organic silica, which is derived from bamboo or from the herb, horsetail. Unfortunately, the herb also contains a diuretic which can deplete minerals. The bamboo supplement is widely available from practitioners and from health foods stores, and is very effective in binding up and displacing aluminium in the body. After taking the organic supplement in about 8 times the recommended amount for about two weeks, I notice a gradual improvement in my state of mental clarity and memory. After about two months, I seemed to be as cogent and mentally agile as before. After another month I had another hair analysis. This showed my aluminium level had dropped through the floor and was now within normally accepted limits.

Clawing your way out

Taking supplements of organic silica is one method of treating yourself for high levels of aluminium. Another is chelation therapy. 'To chelate' means literally to form a claw. A chelating agent is usually an amino acid or derivative which is used to help the body absorb supplements of inorganic substances such as iron and zinc. It works like a metabolic piggyback, ferrying minerals across the gut lining to deposit them in the blood. However, chelation can work both ways. EDTA, a highly active amino acid, is used to scour the body in a search for toxic heavy metal contaminants, then once it finds them, to latch on to them like a claw and eject them before they can do any further damage. As well as tracking down toxins such as lead it is also excellent at getting rid of aluminium. Unfortunately, the vigour with which EDTA eradicates toxins is also its failing since it will throw the metabolic baby out with the bathwater: zinc levels, for example, are particularly vulnerable to EDTA. This chelator is injected directly into the bloodstream. Because of its effects on benign minerals as well as bad it should be administered only under the strictest supervision.

This chapter has shown you how to systematically and actively take the initiative in removing many of the most common sources of aluminium from your life. The advice it contains may prove to be a valuable insurance policy that will bear fruit in later life. It may, on the other hand, prove in years to come to be simply misguided and ill-informed ramblings. Ultimately, whether you choose to follow our advice – whether you put up with considerable inconveniences and possibly higher living expenses – is up to you. At least be thankful that you have that choice.

Because, for some people, the choice has been wrested irretrievably out of their hands. For whatever reason they have already fallen victims to the hopeless, progressive mental and physical degradation of Alzheimer's disease. In the next and final chapter we'll see how relatives learn to cope with such trying circumstances and look at the support they can expect to receive from the organizations set up to help them.

10

Living with Alzheimer's Disease

Alzheimer's disease changes the lives of those who must care for its victims in a deeper and more dramatic fashion than any other disease. Certainly, looking after a victim of Alzheimer's disease can be a physically draining, thankless, aggravating, frustrating and infuriating experience. And these negative feelings are compounded by the fact that it is currently incurable, its progress, no matter how erratic, unstoppable. Yet many diseases are terminal, so why should this one in particular be any worse? The answer is that most severely debilitating illnesses, no matter how traumatic, leave their victims largely in possession of their faculties. Their sense of reason remains and with it the ability to communicate and share their distress with others. Often this communication becomes an umbilical cord through which a great deal of the suffering can be alleviated, small triumphs lingered upon and morale raised. The very nature of Alzheimer's disease, on the other hand, severs this vital communication cord.

As the ravages of Alzheimer's becomes more pronounced, communication and understanding between carer and cared for diminishes. There ceases to be that common ground of shared experience that so often seems miraculously to transform the trial of coping with disability into an uplifting triumph of human spirit.

So does Alzheimer's leave no room for hope? Does it mean that the carer will be subjected to a downward spiral of unending, unacknowledged misery? Not a bit of it! Of course the disease is a terrible blight in the way it arbitrarily cuts down relatives and loved ones. Yes, it does have to be endured by carers – usually close relatives – with heroic, possibly thankless, efforts that go largely unsung. Yes, too, its effects are progressive and irreversible.

Despite all this, much hope can be salvaged from this seemingly hopeless situation. For the victim, his or her life can be made as uncomplicated and secure as possible, their increasingly erratic and vulnerable emotional state soothed in an atmosphere of love and patience. For the carers, the seemingly monumental task of looking after the victim can be achieved by a considered and systematic planning of their lives. Routines can be established, measured responses to the victim's behaviour decided in advance and then acted upon. In this way the traumas, and the carers' reactions to them, can be anticipated and overcome, hidden strengths and talents brought to light and the calmest, most sustaining atmosphere for all concerned nurtured.

For the carer, achieving this ideal means coming to terms with some hard facts – both about the nature of dementia and his or her own character. Let's see what these facts are:

The decline into dementia

Alzheimer's disease is very erratic. The dementia which it causes can be described clinically as a progressive decline in the victim's ability to think, reason, remember and learn. Within this broad, bland summation, the pattern of the disease will vary in intensity and speed of progress from individual to individual. The first signs of the onset of Alzheimer's disease are hardly detectable. Indeed, it is often only when the victim's close friends or relations analyse his or her behaviour retrospectively that any suggestion of illness becomes detectable at all.

Early symptoms will include lethargy and apathy; a marked unwillingness to experience new things such as a different food or new holiday destination; indeciveness; a tendency to heap the blame onto others for such things as missed appointments, broken ornaments or disagreements over trivial matters; an inability to grasp quickly new ideas such as driving directions or weather forecasts; self centredness; and mild repetitiousness. Most of us have these characteristics to a greater or lesser extent and, since the incipient victim might not exhibit them all, it is obviously very difficult to recognize the onset of the disease when it occurs.

Not so the second, so-called moderate dementia, stage. By

now the sufferer has become forgetful of recent events and more hazy about recall of past ones; time has become distorted, ceasing to have any real meaning so that the victim might go out shopping in the dead of the night and, once out, quickly become lost; one member of the family will be confused for another; gas rings will be turned on then left unlit, cigarettes and fires left burning and unattended; both personal hygiene and meals will be neglected even though the victim will later insist that he or she has washed and eaten; the victim could well become clinging and slightly pitiful; and they might start to suffer from hallucinations.

The final, severest stage of dementia often leaves victims without any sense of cogency at all. They constantly repeat themselves; they need help with straightforward physical tasks such as bathing and getting dressed; they may undress at inopportune moments such as in public; they may be unable to understand what is being said to them; they could become aggressive and violent; they could even lose control of their movements.

Each victim may experience some or all of these symptoms, or even others which we haven't listed. The only constant in this is that it forms a steepening curve of deterioration and that it is characterized by many such variables. Even the victims' abilities will vary from day to day. On occasions they may appear reasonably cogent and aware, as if they have undergone minor remission.

In the face of this, imagine then the enormous anxieties and stresses forcing down on the victims. Succumbing to dementia is not simply a matter of falling into a state of immediate mental oblivion, an instantaneous loss of thoughts and sensibilities. It is a painfully slow decline during which time the victims are aware of what is happening to them, conscious of the progressive loss of clarity, the tantalizing inability to recall important memories. One Alzheimer's patient compared the disease to 'being in a prison whose walls are closing in, getting closer and closer to me'. To lose one's faculties and to be aware of losing them, must be a bewildering and terrifying experience. Is it any wonder that it breeds such powerful resentment, frustration and anger and that, without any other way of articulating these feelings, the victim becomes aggressive and violent?

And what of the carer? Health care resources in Britain are, by any criteria, severely stretched. Increasingly the public is called upon to take the burden of caring for the aged and infirm upon itself. What this means is that chronically ill men and women – often suffering from severe dementia – are now being looked after by individuals whose prior experience of healthcare was probably no more advanced than dishing out the occasional aspirin.

Avoiding the pitfalls

As daunting as this prospect must appear, the challenges it creates can be met and successfully overcome as long as you follow certain guidelines and avoid certain pitfalls. Let's see what some of these are:

Guilt avoidance

'The other day I just flew off the handle at him. I'd given him his supper, cut it all up for him because he was behaving fractiously and refusing to make any sort of effort, then went back to the kitchen to fetch my own plate. I was only out of the room for thirty seconds or so but when I came back he was spitting the food on the floor and shouting "yuck", endlessly repeating "yuck" like a spoiled brat of a child. Well I just saw red and went for him. I screamed at him "you stupid bloody idiot, just what the —— do you think you're doing!" I wanted to slap him, to scratch him, to hurt him really badly, to shake him about. I was crying, almost hysterical. I wanted to hurt him yet he just sat there with his eyes rolling and that made it worse.

'Later, when I calmed down, I felt ashamed of myself. I'd wanted to hurt him when, God, he's been hurt so much already. I felt so guilty for my outburst. I just wanted the ground to open up and swallow me. I felt unworthy and incapable.' This is an account from a woman in her late thirties, Val, who is caring for her septuagenarian father, Greg. It graphically illustrates the tensions and forces that conspire to pull a carer in so many directions at once. Val is an intelligent, brave and caring woman, yet even for her the stresses can become too great. Even months later, retelling her story seemed to rekindle the enormous energy that was instantly and uncontrollably unleashed at her father. Several important points about caring for sufferers are raised here but perhaps the most important of all is the need to come to terms with the feelings of guilt.

After attacking her father, Val was overwhelmed with guilt. For days she felt she shouldn't even be trusted to go near him and a home help had to be drafted in to take care of him. It's fair to say that Val's guilt during that time bordered on self-loathing. Certainly, it is true that during her outburst, Val had lost that crucial ability to distinguish between anger at the victim and anger at the dementia. Yet who can blame her? Only herself, it seems. For weeks afterwards she was riddled with guilt.

What good did this guilt do her? Guilt is the worst emotion to feel in this or any circumstance. All it did was undermine her self-confidence, chipping away at her belief in her own considerable ability to look after her father. She became tense, self-critical and, as she now admits, this only fuelled the resentment and anger she felt towards herself. Far from a means of relieving her sense of blame it was making it worse. Guilt, for whatever reason, is wholly negative. It achieves nothing apart from destruction.

Self-awareness, on the other hand, in Val's case a realization that her actions were wrong yet understandable, is positive. Recognizing, then accepting, your mistakes on the one hand, and shrouding yourself in guilt on the other are completely opposite to each other. Guilt ultimately obscures self-awareness. It is a lot easier to feel guilty about an action than it is to analyse that action rationally, coming to terms with your reason for behaving the way you did, then adding it to the sum of your experiences.

In other words, don't ever allow yourself to feel guilty for your shortcomings. Learn from them instead.

Anger

As we've just seen, anger goes hand in hand with guilt and can be just as destructive. Anger at the lack of home care services, anger at the victim's behaviour, anger even at relations who are not giving you the support you feel you deserve. If you allow it, anger will very quickly turn into bitterness and resentment. On the other hand, carefully channelled it can be a galvanizing force for good, breeding a steely determination to get things done. Val's anger was the negative side of the sort of strength and determination that has sustained her for over two years as her father's faculties have declined. Certainly allow yourself to experience your anger. Don't pretend it's not there. But use it creatively. Dash a letter off to your local newspaper complaining about lack of home care services – if it doesn't appear phone up the editor and badger him until it does – or harass the council about providing extra home help.

Speaking your mind

Val admits that one of the reasons for her outburst is that she doesn't often get the chance to express her anxieties to others. Thus, in the words of the Americans, she 'internalizes' too much, allowing frustrations to build up inside her like a pressure cooker. Talking about your feelings to a friendly ear is immensely important. Val's particular worries include the sense of disjointedness created by the role reversal – once her father took care of her, wiping her mouth after eating, clearing up after her messes, now the situations are uncannily reversed. Another cause of stress is the never quite acknowledged, but never wholly denied, sense that her father might make a recovery. Minute signs of clarity are taken for symptoms of remission and when it proves to be a false hope, the disappointment can be crushing.

Val says that she 'felt guilty about boring a friend with my problems'. If that person is a true friend, they won't object to talking about it. And even in the unlikely event that they do object, then it's up to them to tell you, not for you to feel guilty on their behalf. We've already agreed that guilt is a self-indulgent, unaffordable luxury. Get rid of it.

Lead your own life

Caring for a demanding Alzheimer's disease victim can occupy most of your waking time. This means that social activity is also often 'internalized', especially if the carer is sustaining his or her efforts alone. Yet regardless of how demanding the victim is, it's crucial that the carer nurtures their own interests, finding time to carry on with activities completely outside the realm of the sufferer. Free time can be provided by sending the sufferer temporarily to a short term residential centre or a hospital, or even having a sitting service visit the home. Details of the different services available can be obtained from the Alzheimer's Disease Society (address at the end of the chapter).

Contact with children

A divorcee, Val has two girls, one aged fourteen and one aged nine. The older child is at that age when she finds spending time in the company of someone exhibiting unusual behaviour acutely embarrassing. The younger daughter, however, enjoys a happy and relaxed relationship with Greg, exhibiting a natural warmth that is returned in full. Alzheimer patients respond positively to the uninhibited company of children and, unless prone to violent and erratic behaviour, this sort of contact should be encouraged.

Sexuality

Because Greg and Val are father and daughter the problem of sexual relations doesn't arise. It does, however, plague many relationships. It's perfectly natural, if the carer is the victim's spouse, for him or her to experience a need for contact and warmth from their partner. Again, many people undergo torments of guilt for having such feelings yet, given the obvious constrictions, there's no reason why spouse and sufferer shouldn't enjoy a fulfilling physical relationship. Alzheimer victims are very sensitive to body language and are easily startled by abrupt movements. Therefore, it's up to the carer to guide the sufferer through their physical encounters with slow, gentle, reassuring movements.

Establishing a routine

'At first it was hopeless,' says Mary of caring for her husband, Phil. 'I tried to make his life as varied as possible, thinking that if the routine was broken up it would help him to concentrate better and make him more alert. So we ate at different times, sat at different spaces at the table, watched television from different chairs even. It didn't work. All it did was confuse and frighten him. If I sat him down at a different table setting he'd get restless and refuse to eat.'

Abandoning this policy on the advice of a health visitor, Mary slowly evolved a structured routine for her and Phil to follow. 'We eat at the same time and in the same places, he helps me with certain jobs around the home, vacuuming, hanging out the washing to dry and so on with each one following the next in an order that never changes from day to day.' Although this might sound stifling, Mary claims that creating a routine like this provides Phil with a secure, consoling way of life within which a remarkable amount of spontaneity is allowed to flourish.

One of the most important points in caring for an Alzheimer's disease victim is to help them retain their skills. In their daily routine, one of Phil's responsibilities is to make the beds. Although he is severely demented, Mary never helps him get dressed or use a knife and fork unless he gets into major difficulty. Throughout the day, Mary provides a spoken commentary of what the two of them are doing, gently reminding and encouraging him, prodding him into meeting each new challenge. 'At times he does get frustrated and angry. I still haven't reached the stage where I can take his abuse on the chin and not feel hurt by it. Perhaps it's better that I never do.'

If one theme emerges from these examples it is about the way hope can be nurtured in the most inhospitable-seeming environment. This is no small achievement since the outcome of Alzheimer's disease is more certain than the results of a diagnosis of cancer. Yet, in remarkable situations people achieve remarkable goals. As far as the disease is concerned, an organization that exists to support carers and victims as they reach for those goals is the Alzheimer's Disease Society. Its stated aims are: to provide support to families by linking them through membership; to educate affected families, carers and the general public of the nature of the disease; to provide carers with as much information as possible on the aid, services and resources available both from government bodies and voluntary organizations; to ensure that carers and victims receive all the support they need – from assessment and diagnosis to provision of residential and hospital care.

For more information write to:

Alzheimer's Disease Society
Mrs Noreen Siba
158-160 Balham High Road
London SW12 9BN
(Tel: 081 675 6557/8/9/0).

Alzheimer's Disease and Related Disorders Association
Edward Truschke
70 East Lake Street
Suite 600
Chicago
IL 60601
USA
(Tel: 312 853 3060).

Alzheimer's Disease and Related Disorders Society
Bryan Moss
PO Box 470
Hawthorn (Tel: 02 805 0100)
Victoria 3122
Australia
(Tel: 03 818 0738).

Branches in different states:

NSW – PO Box 139, Ryde NSW 2112
(Tel: 02 805 0100)
VIC – 84 Eastern Road, South Melbourne VIC 3205
(Tel: 03 696 1696)
QLD – PO Box 446, Lutwyche QLD 4030
(Tel: 07 857 4043)
TAS – (Hobart) 2 St John's Avenue, Newtown TAS 7008
(Tel: 002 28 189)
(Launceston) c/o 185 Penquisite Road, Norwood
TAS 7250 (no phone)
SA – PO Box 202, Eastwood SA 5063 (Tel: 08 373 2670)
WA – c/o Homes of Peace, Subiaco WA 6008
(Tel: 09 388 2800)

Conclusion

Mind and Body, Consciousness and Memory

In common with many others, Arthur Koestler, novelist and one of this century's greatest scientific polyglots, believed that humankind suffers from a physical flaw that will, in time, prove fatal. This flaw he identified as an imperfect joining in the brain between its two main components – the cortex and the lower brain. To understand what he meant it is helpful to look at each component briefly in turn.

Refined, reasoned and classified

The cortex is the higher part of our brains. Receiving sensory input from the millions of nerve endings around the body, it defines them and illuminates them, creating fathomable certainties from the mêlée and chaos of the world around us. Split into two hemispheres, it determines our characteristics and personalities as well as creating modes of thought. It helps us, say, to identify a colour, then narrow it down to a specific shade and hue. It then enables us to respond to that colour intellectually, descriptively, poetically and scientifically.

The cortex works by breaking apart the mass of sensory input and categorizing it into separate compartments. It is the cortex that gives us the language we need to communicate and the reason and memory we need to be able to construct that language. It allows us to perceive, question, act upon and discard the myriad shards of information we absorb every second.

The cortex can achieve all this because it has a wonderfully evolved classification mechanism. Rather than receiving information en masse throughout the entire cortex, different regions are designated to receive different forms of sensory input. These regions are called the somatic sensory areas. Lying crossways through both hemispheres of the cortex, together these regions receive information from the entire body. (Interestingly, each half of the cortex receives its input from points on the opposite side of the body.)

Some of the regions of the somatic cortex seem to receive a disproportionately large amount of information from certain points. The lips, for example, represent the greatest single area, followed by the face and the thumbs. The reason for this is that the space in the cortex given to receiving input from a particular part of the body is directly proportionate to the number of receptors to be found in that part. Therefore, while a massive number of sensory nerve endings are concentrated in areas such as the thumbs and lips, very few are to be found in an area such as the skin of the trunk.

In other parts of the cortex, too, individual functions have been tracked down. Experiments using electrical stimulation on different parts of the cortex have revealed a remarkable degree of specialization in certain areas. Memory patterns, voluntary motor impulses (the messages that cause our muscles to contract and relax when we want to move), eye turning, elaboration of thought, speech and vision can all be traced to individual areas of the brain in much the same way as the sensory receptors of the somatic region can.

When you think how much information you have to absorb each day – a kaleidoscope of potentially bewildering images, sounds, impressions, tactile encounters, smells – the ability of the cortex to refine it all into easily managed sense or order means that it can almost be looked upon as a 'reason organ'. Not so the lower brain.

Passionate, primitive and disordered

The lower brain includes a number of separate components such as the thalamus, the hypothalamus, rhinencephalon and reticular formation. Unlike the cortex, it is concerned with crude emotional responses such as pleasure and comfort and powerful physical sensations such as pain and sexual arousal. In contrast to the cortex, the lower brain could well be described as the 'instinct organ'. It has no capacity for perceiving anything but the crudest messages and triggering a strong emotional reaction in response.

This lower region is sometimes called the reptilian brain. In ancestry, it extends hundreds of millions of years further back along the evolutionary trail than the cortex – back in fact to our lizard forebears. It is concerned with survival, with gut responses to stressful situations. The reasoning, classifying cortex evolved later as an appendage to this reptilian brain. Today each serves a vital function, the lower brain responding to sensory input before channelling it on up to the cortex. However, it was Arthur Koestler's contention that somehow, somewhere along the line, the growth of the cortex onto the lower brain went catastrophically wrong.

Out of our minds

Ideally, the reasoning, perceptive cortex should work hand in glove with the instinctiveness of the lower brain. Indeed, in many circumstances it does just that – allowing humankind to marry the irrational flights of fancy of the thalamus with the analytical processes of the cortex and resulting in monumental human inspiration. The theory of relativity, the discovery that the world is spherical, the painting of the *Nightwatch*, all owe their existence to this balance between reason and emotion. However, for every one example of creative impulses there are ten examples of its destructive alternative – relativity led to the creation of the atom bomb, for instance, Galileo was threatened with being burnt at the stake unless he repented his heresies, and so on. All the evidence suggests that the balance there is very shaky indeed. How else are we to account for the cataclysmic wars over the centuries, the willingness of humans to subdue their fellows under the guises of religious belief or sovereignty or geography? How, indeed, are we to justify global economics based on market forces which cause poverty and starvation when the means, if well marshalled, clearly exist to make everybody's life comfortable? How are we to justify rancorous political divisions, and the blind hatred of the football hooligan or the Ku Klux Klansman? And how else are we to explain obsession with the duality of our natures as expressed in the creation of mythical figures such as Dr Jekyll and Mr Hyde and Star Trek's

Mr Spock, his battle between logic and emotion forever played out before us? Reason is submerged and perverted by emotion. Yet emotion empowers our reason to achieve truly fantastic aims. This is the human race's greatest dilemma. And the prognosis for a solution is not good.

So what does this have to do with memory? Everything. Because it is when we look at the way our memories operate that the endless tension between upper and lower brain becomes most apparent. The sudden, profound emotions of sadness and joy generated by memories (such as those of the salesman Oliver in Chapter 1) and the embarrassing mistakes of so-called Freudian slips both point to the lower brain forcing its way up into the cortex's territory. And what of a loss of memory? When Alzheimer's disease, stroke, virus or injury destroys the reasoning, learning and remembering functions of the cortex, the emotional functions of the lower brain are often released with a vengeance. Some of the commonest symptoms of dementia and chronic amnesia, after all, are aggression, anger and emotional instability.

If all this sounds rather depressing, let's end with an upbeat note of optimism. The function of memory is to help us learn. By learning we can recognize the mistakes both of ourselves and of others. This in turn can lead to a degree of self-awareness, an ability, if we choose to use it, effectively to step back from ourselves and rationally take stock of our lives. In a world of such rampant irrationality, this is a pretty marvellous thing to be able to do.

Index

By the same authors:

Fats, Nutrition and Health

Fat is one of the most widely misunderstood of all food substances. In the public mind it is associated with obesity, cardio-vascular disease, diabetes and cancer. Yet there are many different varieties of fats, which perform different functions. Some are inert, and just impose an extra load on the body, whereas others are some of the most biochemically active substances on earth, and as such are vital to human health. Indeed, some work has been done on the link between essential fatty acids and heart health. More confusion is created by the food industry, which likes to proclaim that its products are high in healthy polyunsaturated fats – but the way these are processed often destroys much of their vitality.

Fats, Nutrition and Health penetrates the marketing hype and looks at the facts, establishing which fats are good, and which are bad, and how consumption of good fats can be increased. Dismissing the widely held view of fat as a killer, it shows how, carefully used, fats can be key components of life, and vital in the fight against disease.

This book is a complete reference work on fats and their relation to nutrition and health. It is suitable for all those who employ nutritional therapy in their practices and those with a keen interest in nutrition, whether as health professionals or as members of the general public who are concerned about what they eat. In particular, it explains:

- the meaning of terms such as polyunsaturate, lipid, triglyceride and phosphatide
- the relationship of fat with carbohydrate and cholesterol
- how fats are used in the billions of chemical reactions that provide energy and structure in the body every day
- how the essential fats can be used to enhance health and vitality – and the biochemical mechanisms through which they work
- how food processing destroys good fat and creates bad, and the way this leads to fat-related illness
- why butter is better than margarine
- why fish oil, evening primrose oil and flax oil should be essential components of everyone's diet

Of further interest:

Nutritional Influences on Illness
A sourcebook of clinical research
Melvyn R. Werbach MD

A basic reference book for every health professional's desk.

- 93 chapters, each summarizing the nutritional literature for a specific illness.
- Six appendices to help guide the clinician towards making appropriate assessments and interventions.
- Thousands of clinical studies abstracted with the emphasis on double-blind experimental studies whenever available.
- Introductory overviews of the longer chapters to ensure that the most essential information is quickly available.
- A detailed index to permit rapid location of information on particular nutrients.
- Includes studies reporting negative results to provide a balanced perspective on the literature.
- Includes coverage of the literature on food sensitivities and toxics.

'A major advance in the field of nutritional medicine . . . This book should be in the hands of every practising physician, as it provides the source material on the clinical relevance of nutrition in the management of so many common diseases for which drug treatment has proved to be non-curative, inadequate and/or dangerous.' – Stephen Davies, MA, BM, B.Ch., founding Chairman of The British Society for Nutritional Medicine and co-author of *Nutritional Medicine*.